Karen Calvin 84'

MVFOL

D0506678

the Wilton way to Decorate for Christmas

EDITED BY EUGENE T. AND MARILYNN C. SULLIVAN

OTHER WILTON BOOKS

The Wilton Way of Cake Decorating, Volume One
The Wilton Way of Cake Decorating, Volume Two
The Wilton Way of Cake Decorating, Volume Three
Beautiful Bridal Cakes the Wilton Way
Discover the Fun of Cake Decorating
The Wilton Book of Wedding Cakes
Modern Cake Decorating
The Wilton Way of Making Gum Paste Flowers
Celebrate! Omnibus
Celebrate! II
Celebrate! III
Celebrate! IV
Celebrate! V
Celebrate! VI
The Complete Wilton Book of Candy
Celebrate! Christmas

Published in 1976. All rights reserved. No part of the contents
of this book may be reproduced without the written consent
of the publisher, Wilton Enterprises, Inc., 2240 West 75th
Street, Woodridge, Illinois 60517.

Library of Congress Catalog Card Number: 76-16083
International Standard Book Number: 0-912696-07-9
Library of Congress Cataloging in Publication Data
Main entry under title:

The Wilton way to decorate for Christmas
    1. Christmas cookery.   2. Christmas decorations.
I. Sullivan, Eugene T.   II. Sullivan, Marilynn.
III. Wilton Enterprises, Inc.
TX739.W54   745.59'41   76-16083
ISBN 0-912696-07-9

WILTON BOOK DIVISION
NORMAN WILTON, Publisher; EUGENE T. and MARILYNN C. SULLIVAN,
Co-editors; MICHAEL NITZSCHE, Senior Decorator; AMY ROHR, GUADALUPE
DE DOMANI, Decorators; BECKY HINES, Assistant Decorator; VIRGINIA
COLWELL, MELISSA RENCKLY, Copy Editors; SANDY LARSON, CAROL
ZALESKI, Art Assistants; DIANE KISH, Reader's Editor; EDWARD
HOIS, Photography; CHEF LUTZ OLKIEWICZ, Pastry and candy consultant;
CULINARY ARTS INSTITUTE, Recipe testing and food preparation.

Printed and bound in Italy by Plurigraf - Narni - Terni

SEVENTH PRINTING SEPTEMBER, 1983

This book
is dedicated to all of you
who keep Christmas merrily and well. Here
you'll find fresh new ideas to inspire you in your
own creative efforts to bring pleasure to others in
this, the happiest season of the year. ☆ Browse through
the bright pages to discover new ways to interpet the
old traditions of good food, festively presented, rooms
trimmed with color and light, and the Christmas tree
decorated more gloriously than ever with ornaments
you and your family make yourselves. ☆ We've in-
cluded all the patterns and instructions you'll
need for these joyous projects. ☆ Most especially,
this book is for children, for Christmas is
the festival of a Child, and of all those
with a childlike heart. ☆
Merry Christmas!

Enlarge patterns. Each square equals 1″

FOR MORE THAN A THOUSAND YEARS green trees have been identified with the celebration of Christmas, the Feast of the Nativity of Christ. Historians believe evergreens came to be used as symbols of *life without end* during the eighth century. At that time St. Boniface is reputed to have dedicated the fir tree to the Holy Child. Christmas trees have since been trimmed to express a wide variety of interesting customs and traditions throughout the world.

Here are suggestions for creating an entirely new collection of ornaments from such workable materials as bread dough, icing, molded sugar and jewel-bright candies. Use them imaginatively to trim a dramatic tree of your very own.

TRIM A TREE WITH GAY FIESTA STARS

To make these unique ornaments, we chose warm reds and yellows. Create your effect in bright primary colors, or the scheme you like best. Whatever colors you choose, the effect will be equally striking.

To make them, you'll need wax paper, sheets of stiff cardboard, short lengths of fine wire, airplane glue, decorating bags, and four cups royal icing tinted with food colors. You will need a tube 13 for each color. Only royal icing will harden to make strong long-lasting shapes.

Before starting ornaments, practice making stars. Hold decorating bag straight up, perpendicular to work surface. Press gently until icing flows out in star shape. Stop pressure and lift bag. Keep a steady motion, making stars as close together as possible.

1. Fill decorating bags with each of the colors you plan to use. Keep tips of tubes covered with a damp cloth when not in use. Enlarge patterns and tape to cardboard. Tape wax paper over them as smoothly as possible.

2. Outline each design with tube 13 stars, then fill in each color area with more stars, covering pattern entirely. Complete each ornament before going on to the next to assure strong, even drying.

3. Allow ornaments to dry thoroughly, at least 24 hours. Peel off paper and turn over. Glue a small loop made of a 2″ length of wire to the back of each ornament. For fast drying, use airplane glue.

4. Pipe back of ornament same as front, covering it completely with tube 13 stars. When the holidays are over, store ornaments carefully. They will last for many Christmases to come.

Six New
and
Beautiful
Tree
Trims

QUAINT
ORNAMENTS
FROM
BREAD DOUGH

CREATE A CHARMING, OLD-FASHIONED TREE this year with bread dough ornaments. The whole family will have fun making these whimsical Christmas trims with a home-spun touch.

Here's what you'll need: one or more batches of bread dough, rolling pin and cookie cutters in your favorite shapes. We used star, sun, moon, snowflake, teddy bear, horse, bird and Christmas tree cutters, each about 3″ to 4″ high. You'll also need aluminum foil and cookie sheets. Other essentials are a sharp knife, an artist's brush, toothpicks, decorating tubes 12, 14, 25, 33 and 34, clear acrylic spray glaze, 4″ lengths of fine wire for hanging the ornaments and colorful ribbon bows to conceal the wire.

BREAD DOUGH RECIPE

2½ cups all-purpose flour
1¼ cups salt
1¼ cups water

Combine flour and salt in large bowl. Add all the water and mix until dough is very stiff. Turn out onto floured counter top or bread board and knead six to eight minutes, until it attains a pliable consistency. Dough is now ready to use. If it is not to be used immediately, dough can be stored in plastic bag in refrigerator for several days. During damp weather, keep it as airtight as possible. If dough dries out, pat on a few drops of water and knead to original consistency. If too sticky, add flour by the tablespoon, kneading until dough stops sticking. This recipe will make about fifty-two 4″ ornaments. *Do not double recipe.* Make another batch, if needed.

1. Roll out dough 1/16″ to 1/8″ thick. It is not necessary to flour the board or rolling pin unless dough begins to stick. If so, dust rolling pin lightly. Using cookie cutters, cut out shapes for ornaments.

2. With spatula, transfer cut-out shapes to foil-covered, ungreased cookie sheets.

3. Now for the fun of decorating! With your hands, roll thin spaghetti-like strips and tiny balls of dough and arrange in various trims. For circles, poke holes in balls of dough with tip of brush handle. For impressions or a textured look, use decorating tubes or sharp knife. "Glue" pieces together by brushing each with water, then pressing together. Add a loop of dough for hanging. Open shapes and ornaments with holes need no loops. Pieces can also be shaped by hand on foil-covered cookie sheets.

Dough art is very personal and creative. After you have the "feel" of the dough, you'll discover many new ways of shaping it.

4. Bake ornaments in preheated 300° oven for about half an hour. Very thin pieces may bake faster, so watch to see they're not too brown. Thick pieces may require longer baking time. If pieces puff up, or are extra-thick, puncture with pin to let air out.

5. When pieces have baked and cooled, spray both sides with clear acrylic glaze. Let dry, then spray again. Glazed ornaments will keep for years. Insert wires in holes for hanging. Glue on tiny ribbon bows after they're hung on the tree.

Dazzling

8

Table-top Trees

Trim a tree with "jewels"
or lacy pastel filigree.
Directions are on pages 10 and 11.

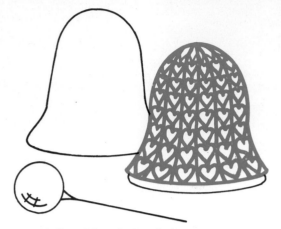

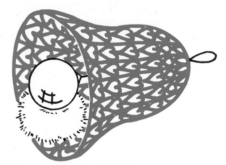

Grease bell mold and pipe design

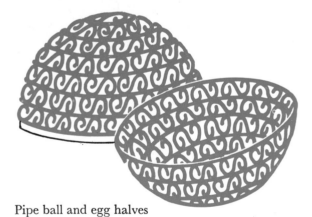

Unmold, insert wire and ball

Pipe ball and egg halves

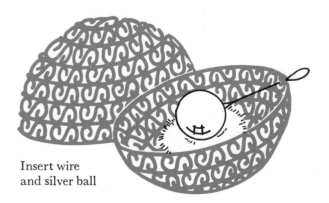

Insert wire
and silver ball

LACY FILIGREE
TRIMS A BREATHTAKING TREE

These elegant filigree ornaments for your Christmas tree are not as difficult to make as you may think, but they do take time to prepare and care to assemble. Here are simple directions for creating airy filigree bell, egg and ball-shaped ornaments. Each requires only icing and a delicate touch. Inside each is an added subtle accent, a shiny silver ball.

Here are the materials you'll need: 2″ and 2½″ Bell Molds, 3″ Ball and Egg Molds, small silver balls, decorating tube 2, small balls of cotton, food coloring, 2½ cups royal icing made with egg white, fine white cloth-covered wire, shortening to coat the molds and decorating bags.

1. Start with bell molds. Grease outside of molds with shortening. Working from the bottom up, pipe tube 2 freehand designs. You can repeat circles, scrolls, hearts, herringbone stripes or lace patterns, just be sure to make the rim about ⅛″ above bottom of mold to permit unmolding. Leave about ¼″ opening at top of bell to insert wire.

2. Allow bell to dry thoroughly. Place bell in warm oven about ½ minute to melt shortening. Slip mold out and let ornament harden, round side up. Push a 6″ length of wire into ring on silver ball and twist end into loop to hold it securely. Twist the other end into a loop and insert this through hole in top of bell. Pipe several lines of royal icing across hole to fill the opening and anchor the wire at center. Prop silver ball with cotton and rest bell on its side, with more cotton under the top loop. Let dry at least four hours.

3. Make ball and egg-shaped ornaments in two pieces. Use only the top rounded half of each egg mold, as bottom half has flat base. Lightly grease outside of egg and ball molds and pipe tube 2 designs freehand, again leaving about ⅛″ between designs and rim of mold. After drying, place in warm oven about ½ minute to melt shortening. Slip mold out and let ornament halves harden, round side up.

4. Insert ball, put halves together. Push a 6″ piece of wire through ring on silver ball, twist one end to hold it securely and loop the other end. Lay it in place inside one half of a filigree egg or ball, with the loop extending outside. Prop ball with cotton. Pipe a line or two of royal icing across wire where it touches edge of egg or ball. Let dry thoroughly, at least four hours. Then remove cotton, pipe line of icing around edge or egg or ball, press halves together and set aside to dry overnight.

5. After ornaments are completed, thread loops with a 4″ length of wire and twist wires onto tree branch.

"JEWELED" ORNAMENTS FOR A DAZZLING TREE

Here's a stunning and original new look for a little tree. Bejewel it with shiny bright Hard Candy Ornaments. Use ruby and amethyst, rose-pink and vibrant orange, colors that will give new holiday sparkle to your home.

In addition to the recipe below, you will need cookie sheets, aluminum foil, a deep, straight-sided 2½ or 3 quart saucepan, a pastry brush, candy thermometer, fine wire and vegetable oil to grease the molds. You will also need Hard Candy Molds in Stars and Shapes and Christmas Figures.

HARD CANDY RECIPE

2 cups granulated sugar
⅔ cup water
¼ teaspoon cream of tartar
Food coloring (by the drop as needed)
1 teaspoon Hard Candy Flavor (optional)

Combine water, sugar and cream of tartar in saucepan and bring to a boil over high heat, stirring constantly. When it begins to boil, stir in coloring, then insert candy thermometer and stop stirring. Continue cooking over high heat, occasionally wiping sides of pan and thermometer with wet pastry brush.

It will take 12 to 15 minutes for candy to cook, but check thermometer often. When it reaches 280°, turn down to low heat or candy will burn. At this stage, stir in flavoring, as it evaporates if added sooner. When candy reaches 300° remove from heat and pour into greased molds.

Each recipe makes enough candy to fill both molds, a total of 16 ornaments. To make more, repeat rather than doubling the recipe. Too big a batch makes the pan too heavy for easy pouring, also the candy tends to solidify before it can all be poured.

1. Fill molds. Lightly grease molds with vegetable oil. Place them on foil-lined cookie sheets. Pour hot syrup into molds, making sure corners are filled.

2. Unmold, add wires. Let candy cool about 15 minutes in refrigerator, or until it hardens. To remove, turn molds upside-down and pop candy out by pressing back of molds lightly with thumbs.

3. To attach hangers, make loops of fine wire about 4″ long, dip each one into a batch of clear hard candy syrup (same recipe without color). Working quickly, dip loops into syrup and place them on backs of ornaments. For extra strength, cover each loop with more syrup, dropped from a small dowel rod or popsicle stick. Let dry about 15 minutes before hanging on tree. Ornaments can be stored flat in a cool, dry place.

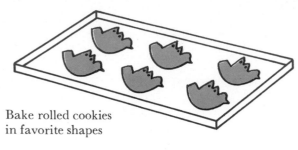

Bake rolled cookies
in favorite shapes

Outline each cookie
with tube 1

Fill in with thinned
royal icing

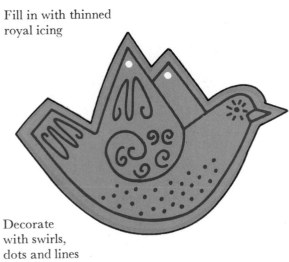

Decorate
with swirls,
dots and lines

MOST CHRISTMASY OF ALL
A COOKIE TREE

If cookies spell Christmas at your house, how about trimming a tree with them? Baking Christmas cookies by the dozen is a warm-hearted tradition that's fun to extend to tree-trimming. Let the whole family join in creating king-size cookie ornaments for your tree.

You will need one or more batches of cookie dough, 4½ cups royal icing, food colors, soda straws, cookie sheets, large spatula, toothpicks, decorating bags and wire for hanging the ornaments. All decorating is done with tube 1.

We used Really Big Cookie Cutters, 5″ to 6″ across, for dramatic effect, but you can use any of your favorite shapes.

ROLL-OUT COOKIES

1¼ cups butter
2 cups sugar
2 eggs
5 cups flour
2 teaspoons baking powder
1 teaspoon salt
½ cup milk
¼ teaspoon grated orange peel

Cream butter and sugar together, then add eggs and beat until fluffy. Sift dry ingredients together and add alternately to creamed mixture with milk. If mixture is too sticky, add a little more flour so that it is easy to handle. Roll dough ¼″ thick and cut. With a soda straw, poke hole in top of each cookie for hanging. We made two holes in the angel, hand, star and bird cookies for easier hanging. Lift cookies with large spatula and place on ungreased cookie sheet.

Bake in 375° oven for eight minutes or until edges are light golden brown. This makes about four dozen large cookies. For a greater number, make additional batches rather than doubling or tripling the recipe.

1. Outline each cookie with a tube 1 line of royal icing, about ¹⁄₁₆″ in from the edge.

2. Thin royal icing with a little water and fill decorating bag. Do not use a tube, just cut off the tip of bag. Flow in icing to cover each cookie, out to the line at the edge.

3. Let coating dry about one hour until it forms a hard crust. Now outline and trim the cookies in bright-colored icing using tube 1 to create fanciful swirls, dots and lines. When trim dries, insert wires in holes and hang the cookies on your tree!

TRIM THE TREE
WITH CANDY IN SUGAR BASKETS

Here's a sweet idea for trimming the Christmas tree —adorn it with miniature baskets of candy. Dainty but durable, these sparkling sugar baskets are so easy to make that even the children can help.

You'll need plastic molds in Bell, Egg and Ball shapes, stiff cardboard, spatula and an icepick for making the baskets. For decorating, you'll need 2 cups royal icing and decorating tubes 2, 10, 13, 14, 15 and 22. Purchase small candies to fill the baskets and ribbon or gilt-covered wire for handles.

SUGAR MOLD RECIPE

2½ pounds granulated sugar
1 egg white
2 or 3 drops of food color

Stir egg white lightly with a fork before mixing with sugar and food color. This mixture resists crumbling and is best for making hollowed-out items. This makes thirty ornaments. Repeat the recipe for each color desired.

Make a sugar star for the treetop! Mold sugar mixture in Star Mold, let dry five hours. Turn over and "glue" a loop of wire to back with royal icing. Trim with bright royal icing.

1. Knead mixture with hands about a minute until well blended. Add a drop or two more food color if tints are too pale.

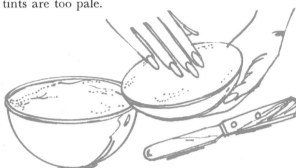

2. Pack sugar mixture into mold as firmly as possible. If making more than four shapes with the same mold, dust mold with cornstarch to prevent sticking. Scrape off excess sugar with spatula making top perfectly flat and level with edge ·

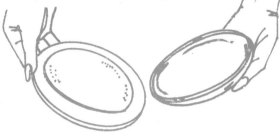

3. Unmold at once. Place cardboard over mold, turn it upside down, lift plastic mold off. Allow to dry for about two hours.

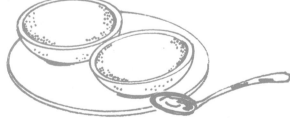

4. Now, **carefully pick up** the sugar mold and hold it in the palm of your hand. Scoop out the soft sugar inside with a teaspoon, leaving a shell about ¼" thick. Set aside until thoroughly dry. Make hole in either side of sugar molds with heated icepick.

5. **Decorate** the little baskets with gay royal icing. Use tube 2 for stringwork, beads and dots, tube 10 for ribbon swags, tube 15 for shell borders, tube 13 and 14 for stars. To make tassel-like trim on the bottom of some baskets, pipe a tube 10 ball of icing and finish with elongated tube 22 rosette.

The Glorious Christmas Cake

You've decorated the house and trimmed the tree with enchanting ornaments of your own making. Now, turn your hand and your creative talents to spectacular cakes for all those special holiday occasions. It's amazing how many different and delightful things you can do with cake and icing.
Crown a cake with evergreen, circle it with Christmas trees, top it with Santa Clauses. Turn a cake into carolers, candy canes, candles or elves, or transform a tiered wedding cake into a Christmas fantasy with lacy snowflakes. Serve the lovely traditional Bûche de Noël or a fruit cake done in the English style. Here you'll find cakes for every occasion and every holiday theme.

A CAKE WREATHED WITH GREENS BRIGHT WITH ORNAMENTS

For that very special party, bring out this fabulous Ornament Cake, garlanded with pine branches.

You'll need two 10″ round pans, a candle, patterns shown on page 18, food coloring, decorating tubes, 1, 2, 13 and 16, decorating bags, wax paper and cardboard. Make one cup Color Flow, one cup royal, and four cups buttercream icing.

1. First make ornaments, using Color Flow Technique. Repeat the patterns to make nine in all.

COLOR FLOW ICING RECIPE

3 ounces water
1 pound confectioners sugar
2 level tablespoons Color Flow mix

Combine sugar and icing mix, add water, mix five minutes at slow speed. Use at once. Note that beating at slow speed keeps you from beating in too much air. If bubbles form while flowing icing, prick them with a pin while icing is still wet.

Tape patterns to stiff cardboard and tape wax paper over them. Outline designs with tube 1 and icing straight from batch, tinting it as needed. Keep icing covered with damp cloth as it is very fast-drying. Let outline dry about one hour, until crusted. Flow in thinned icing. To soften icing for filling in outlined spaces, place a small amount in container and add water, a few drops at a time, stirring by hand.

To be sure thinned icing flows properly, spoon a "blob" of icing, and let it drop back into container. When it takes a full count of ten to disappear, icing is ready. Never fill decorating bag more than half full of thinned icing. Let each color dry about an hour before flowing in the next. Dry twenty-four hours, peel paper off and pipe details with tube 2.

 2. Make pine needles. Tape wax paper to cardboard, and with tube 2 and royal icing pipe lines as shown at left. Repeat, to make about 300 sets. Dry about three hours.

3. Bake cake. Bake two layers, fill and ice with buttercream. Pipe tube 16 puff border around base. Pipe tube 13 stars between puffs. Top puffs with tube 13 c-shaped scrolls.

4. Place trim on cake. Attach ornaments to side of cake with dots of icing. Pipe tube 2 pine needles all around top edge of cake, extending some onto top and side. Next, position prepared sets of pine needles with dots of icing, layering them to make a thick garland. Push candle into center of cake, and pipe tube 13 shells around base. Serves fourteen.

TREES DO THE TRIMMING
ON THIS CHRISTMAS CAKE

Bedecked with trees, and glowing with candlelight and stars, this Christmas-cheery cake is ideal for informal entertaining during the holidays. Picture it serving as a conversation piece on your Christmas Eve buffet table, starring at a festive dinner, or welcoming carolers back from their Yuletide rounds.

To make this Christmas Tree cake, you need about two tablespoons of Color Flow icing for stars, tree pattern, toothpicks, decorating tubes 1, 6, 15 and 75, an 8″ red taper, two 12″ hexagon cake pans, a foil-covered cake board, food coloring, four cups buttercream icing and decorating bags.

1. Make Color Flow stars. Prepare six ⅞″ stars and two 1½″ stars with Color Flow technique described on page 16. Tape wax paper over patterns on board, outline with tube 1 and flow in icing. Allow to dry.

2. Make cake. Bake two 12″ hexagon cake layers. Fill layers and ice smoothly with buttercream. Place on foil-covered board.

3. Decorate cake. First, pipe "Merry Christmas" on top with tube 1. Pipe tube 6 white ball border around top of cake. To make trees, hold tree pattern against each side panel of cake and trace with toothpick. Fill tree area with tube 15 stars, building layers of star on star in middle of tree to give dimension. Starting at base, pipe tube 75 leaves to make "branches" covering entire tree. Top each tree with a small Color Flow star, attaching with dot of icing. Pipe tube 10 green ball border around base of cake between trees. Insert taper in center of cake top and edge its base with tube 2 beading. Attach two larger stars to candle with dots of icing. Serves twenty.

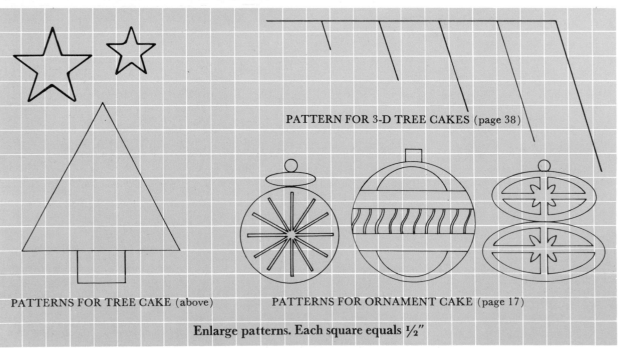

PATTERN FOR 3-D TREE CAKES (page 38)

PATTERNS FOR TREE CAKE (above)   PATTERNS FOR ORNAMENT CAKE (page 17)

Enlarge patterns. Each square equals ½″

SANTA TRIMS A TREE

Let's have a "Trim The Tree Party"! Here's the perfect cake for the occasion, trimmed with six jolly Santas bearing glowing candles. This colorful cake will give a cheerful welcome to your guests, or highlight a holiday buffet.

To make this festive cake, you need wax paper, aluminum foil, stiff cardboard, decorating tubes 1, 16 and 75, decorating bags, and a Christmas Tree pan. You also need food coloring, 1½ cups of Color Flow icing and four cups of buttercream icing.

1. Make Color Flow Santas and star, using technique described on page 16. (Prepare extras in case of breakage.) Tape patterns on cardboard and tape wax paper smoothly over them. Outline everything except the belt with white Color Flow icing. The belt is outlined in brown. Let dry until icing crusts, then flow in thinned icing. Make the star the same way. Allow Color Flow pieces to dry at least forty-eight hours before peeling off paper.

2. Bake cake in Christmas Tree pan. (Pan holds one cake mix.) Cool, and place on foil-covered cardboard cut to tree shape.

3. Decorate cake. Pipe tube 16 stars to cover entire tree, using green for the body of the tree and striping the base in red, orange and yellow. Then cover body of tree with a thick layer of leaves, pulled out with tube 75. Put Santas in position on the tree. Position star on mound of icing. Serves twelve.

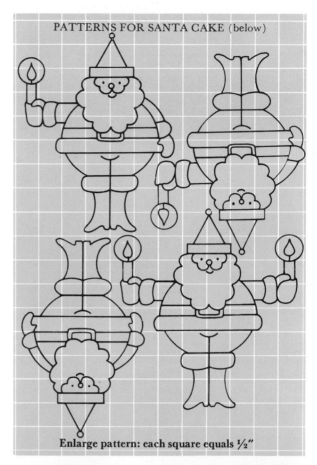

PATTERNS FOR SANTA CAKE (below)

Enlarge pattern: each square equals ½"

Carolers

Bring joy to the table and brighten your holiday buffet with three charming carolers in traditional Victorian dress. Their skirts are cake, the quaint costumes made of icing.

You will need a Large Wonder Mold cake pan, three Little Girl Doll picks, spatula, toothpicks, small pieces of colored construction paper, foil-covered cake boards, food coloring, 6½ cups butter-cream icing, decorator tubes 1, 1s, 2, 3, 13, 14, 16, 48, 104, 124, 127, parchment paper, masking tape, and pen.

To make, bake three cakes in large Wonder Mold pan, cool, and, cover each with thin coat of icing. Place each on a cake board. Cover dolls' hair with masking tape as a base for piping hats, then insert doll picks in cakes. To lengthen waists, insert picks so about ½" of stem is exposed. Smooth icing into gap.

Cut small songbooks from construction paper and letter title of carol on backs with pen. Now you are ready to "dress" your carolers.

Emily wears a warm red coat. Mark a triangle at front of skirt with toothpick and apply blue icing with spatula to fill area. Pipe tube 104 ruffle at base of triangle. Now fill remainder of skirt with tube 14 stars. Cover bodice and arms with tube 13 stars.

Pipe tube 2 cuffs and tube 1 buttons, then trim edge of skirt along triangle with tube 1 beading. To make tabs along coat front, pipe three or four tube 2 lines side by side, brush smooth and shape to a point. Cover hat with tube 14 stars, piping star on star to build up a peaked crown at back. Pipe tube 48 scarf with tube 1 tassels, fringe and trim.

Julia wears a blue coat with matching hat. Mark areas for coat, skirt and stripes with toothpick. Pipe tube 14 zigzags in vertical stripes of blue and green on skirt. Pipe tube 124 ruffle at base of skirt. Then cover bodice, arms and coat areas with tube 13 stars.

Make fur trim on coat hem, collar and cuffs by piping tube 14 stars and covering them with a series of overlapping tube 1 curves. Pipe tube 1 buttons. Build up hat with tube 13 stars, adding star on star at sides. Pipe tube 1 ribbon and bow under chin.

Louisa's caped coat is green with cheery red borders. Outline coat area with toothpick and apply brown icing with spatula around base of skirt and in triangle area. Pipe tube 127 ruffle around bottom of skirt and tube 3 beading above the ruffle. Fill coat from hem to waist with tube 16 stars. Cover bodice and arms with tube 13 stars, piping star on star to extend edge of cape area.

Pipe tube 13 zigzags for border of cape and for cuffs. Pipe tube 13 stars for hood, adding star on star around face to build up that area. Pipe tube 1 bow on hood and tube 1 buttons on coat.

Place songbooks in hands of carolers, securing them with a dab of glue on each hand. Each serves twelve.

AN ELEGANT CHRISTMAS FRUITCAKE IN THE ENGLISH MANNER

One of the most enduring favorites among Christmas desserts is the fruitcake, and here is an especially delicious one. We thank **Helen Wooldridge** of Las Cruces, New Mexico, for this recipe for Best-Ever Applesauce Fruitcake. Firm and moist, it's perfect for decorating in the English style. First the cake is coated with apricot glaze, then marzipan, and given a top layer of fluffy royal icing.

To make, you'll need a double recipe of marzipan (page 52), one 8-ounce jar apricot preserves, a little confectioners' sugar, a sharp knife, spatula, rolling pin, English royal icing, and the following cake.

BEST-EVER APPLESAUCE FRUITCAKE

3 cups all-purpose flour
2 teaspoons baking soda
1 teaspoon baking powder
½ teaspoon cloves
½ teaspoon nutmeg
½ teaspoon cinnamon
½ teaspoon salt
1 pound candied cherries
½ pound mixed candied fruit
1 jar (8 ounces) candied pineapple
¾ cup dates
1 cup raisins
1½ cups pecans
1½ cups walnuts
½ cup butter
1 cup sugar
2 eggs
½ cup grape juice
1½ cups applesauce

1. Sift and mix flour, baking soda, baking powder, spices and salt.

2. Cut up fruit and coarsely chop nuts. Mix the fruit and nuts together.

3. Cream butter and sugar. Add eggs and beat well.

4. Beating until blended after each addition, alternately add dry ingredients and grape juice to the creamed mixture. Mix in fruit, nuts and applesauce.

5. Turn into a greased 9″ x 3″ springform pan and bake at 275° about two and a half hours. Bake rest of batter in a loaf pan.

6. Run a knife around sides of pan and let cake set ten minutes in pan. Remove cake and cool thoroughly. It keeps well for two months or more tightly wrapped and also freezes well.

COVERING THE CAKE

First fill in any holes or crevices in the cake with marzipan, so it has a smooth surface.

1. Dust work surface with confectioners' sugar and roll out a ball of marzipan to a circle ¼″ thick and slightly larger than the diameter of the cake.

2. Brush cake top with warm apricot glaze (heat one jar apricot preserves to boiling and strain). Place cake upside down on marzipan and cut excess edges with knife. With spatula, lift cake and turn upright.

3. Shape remaining marzipan into a long narrow roll and flatten with a rolling pin. Measure, and cut width to equal height of cake, then cut length to exceed circumference slightly.

4. Brush cake sides with apricot glaze. Place sideways on end of marzipan strip and roll, patting marzipan in place until strip ends overlap. Now the cake is ready to be covered with royal icing.

ROYAL ICING

3 egg whites (room temperature)
1 pound confectioners' sugar
1 tablespoon lemon juice

Combine ingredients, beat at high speed seven to ten minutes. This icing is very quick-drying, so keep covered with a damp cloth. Makes 2½ cups.

Cover the cake thickly with the icing, pulling it into points with a spatula. Trim with Christmas candles and holly, real or piped.

BUCHE DE NOEL, FRENCH YULE LOG

In France the traditional Christmas dessert is the Bûche de Noël*. On Christmas Eve, most French families will have a light snack at their usual evening meal time, then attend midnight mass together. Returning from church about one o'clock, the family and very close friends will sit down to a gala supper called "Réveillon". The menu usually includes roast chicken or turkey, baked ham, salad and vegetables, bonbons, wine, and as a climax, the Bûche de Noël. This delectable rolled cake symbolizes the yule log which used to be carried in ceremoniously to burn all the twelve days of Christmas.

This spectacular dessert is not as difficult to make as it may seem, since it can be assembled well in advance. Real holly can be used to trim the cake, or you can pipe holly leaves and berries of regular buttercream icing several days ahead and store in the freezer. On a curved surface, pipe tube 113 leaves, pulling out points with a small damp brush. Add tube 8 berries and freeze.

BASIC SPONGE SHEET

6 eggs, separated
1/4 teaspoon salt
1/2 cup sugar
1 teaspoon vanilla
1/2 cup flour

1. Beat egg whites with salt until they stand in soft peaks. Add four tablespoons sugar, one tablespoon at a time, and continue beating until meringue is very stiff. In a separate bowl beat egg yolks with remaining sugar and vanilla until fluffy.

2. Gently fold about one-fourth of the meringue into egg yolk mixture. Pour back into bowl of meringue. Sprinkle with two tablespoons flour and fold together. Repeat until all the flour is blended. Be careful not to over-mix.

3. Pour into a buttered 12" x 18" jelly roll pan that has been lined with buttered waxed paper. Bake ten to twelve minutes in a 400° oven until golden.

4. Sprinkle a tea towel with confectioners' sugar. As soon as cake is baked, remove it from oven and invert on towel, waxed paper on top. Do not remove waxed paper. Roll cake tightly in towel to an 18" long cylinder, and allow to cool.

5. Carefully unroll cake and peel off waxed paper. Trim off crusty edges and spread cake thinly with Continental Butter Cream, mocha flavored, and thickly with Crème Chantilly. Reroll and refrigerate one-half hour. Cake is now ready to decorate.

CONTINENTAL BUTTER CREAM, MOCHA FLAVORED

A smooth rich concoction used for filling and icing many continental cakes and tortes.

2/3 cup sugar
1/3 cup water
1/8 teaspoon cream of tartar
5 egg yolks
1 cup soft butter
4 ounces semi-sweet chocolate, melted
3 tablespoons extra strong coffee
2 1/2 tablespoons cognac

1. Mix sugar, water, and cream of tartar in saucepan. Stir over low heat until sugar is completely dissolved. Raise heat and boil without stirring until syrup tests 238°.
2. Meanwhile, beat egg yolks in bowl until fluffy. Pour the hot syrup in a thin stream into the yolks, beating constantly. The mixture will become thick and light as it cools from the beating. Set aside until completely cooled. Beat in softened butter a little at a time. Reserve 1/3 cup of Continental Butter Cream to ice ends of the log.
3. To remaining mixture, add melted chocolate, coffee, and cognac and beat in well. Continental Butter Cream can be refrigerated a day or two.

CREME CHANTILLY

1 cup heavy cream
2 tablespoons sugar
1/2 teaspoon vanilla

1. Whip cream, making sure the cream, bowl, and beaters are all very cold. Use an electric mixer on high speed, or a rotary egg beater.
2. Just as the cream begins to thicken, beat in sugar and vanilla. Cover and refrigerate.

DECORATE THE LOG

1. Put Continental Butter Cream, mocha flavored, in decorating bag fitted with tube 17 and pipe long horizontal lines on log to resemble bark. Stop pressure at end of each line to make clean edges. Fill another bag with reserved (unflavored) Butter Cream and pipe tube 17 spirals over ends of cake, starting at center and working out. Do not cover ends of "bark".
2. Attach leaves and berries to log with dots of icing. Refrigerate until serving time. Serves sixteen.

From THE WILTON BOOK OF CLASSIC DESSERTS

A SNOWFLAKE CAKE
FOR A HOLIDAY BRIDE

The crystalline beauty of icing snowflakes enhances this exquisite petite wedding cake designed for a holiday bride. The snowflakes are made with a technique similar to that used in creating the filigree ornaments on page 10.

You will need 10" and 6" round cake pans, 5" Corinthian pillars, 6" separator plates, four ¼" dowel rods, an icepick and stiff white cloth-covered wire. You'll also need food color, decorating tubes 2, 3, 6, 7 and 10, decorating bags, Petite Bridal Couple and Petite Base. Make one cup royal icing for snowflakes and four cups buttercream icing.

1. Make snowflakes. Tape snowflake patterns shown on this page to cardboard or sheet of glass, and tape wax paper over them, smoothing out wrinkles. Outline patterns with royal icing using tube 2. Let some dry on curved surfaces same size as tiers. Flakes to be used on top and between the pillars should be dried flat. When all are dry, overpipe main lines for strength. Let dry again and peel off wax paper.

Attach wire to back of the flat snowflakes with a line of icing, then overpipe backs with tube 2.

2. Bake cakes. Bake two-layer 10" x 4" and 6" x 3" round cakes. Cool, then fill and ice with buttercream icing. Place 10" tier on tray.

3. Assemble cake. Press lower separator plate gently into icing on top of the 10" tier, to make an outline. Remove, and insert dowel rods within the outlined area. Push rods down into cake to tray, lift out and clip off exposed portions. Push back into cake so they are level with top. Punch small hole in center of lower separator plate with heated icepick. Snap pillars onto plate and set on top of the 10" tier. Insert large wired snowflake through hole in plate, so wire will extend into cake. Place 6" tier on other plate and position this on top of the pillars.

4. Decorate cake. Edge lower separator plate with tube 7. Pipe tube 10 ball border around base of 10" tier and tube 7 ball border around its top. Pipe tube 6 ball border around bottom of 6" tier and tube 3 bulb border around the top.

5. Add remaining trim. Attach snowflakes to sides of cake with dots of icing, and position wired snowflakes by inserting wires into top tier. Place bridal couple ornament on top of cake. Serves sixty-four.

The wonderful Wedding Cake

Here is a cake worthy of a Christmas wedding—towering, snow white, graced with winged angels and brightened with poinsettias and evergreens.

Taken step-by-step, and with advance planning, this cake is not difficult to achieve even in the busy days before Christmas. Cake tiers can be baked ahead and frozen, flowers and trees made well in advance.

First get all supplies on hand. You'll need eight plastic Angelinos, separator plates—a 12″ round, 11″ square and two 7″ square—eight 5″ Grecian Pillars, three plates from the Petite Heart base, four 3″ Lace Bells, three Flower Spikes and a Petite Bridal Couple.

Tubes needed are 2, 3, 14, 20, 22, 32, 65 and 74 plus a number 7 nail.

ROYAL ICING FLOWERS AND TREES

1. First make about ninety poinsettias. Attach small square of wax paper to number 7 nail with dot of icing. Using tube 65 start at center of nail and pipe in four even petals. Add four more in between, then a row of eight in center, shorter and pulled up higher. Add tube 1 dots of yellow icing. Dry.

2. Wire flowers and leaves. On a wax paper square, pipe a small green icing mound with tube 3. Insert green florist's wire 4″ long into mound and brush smooth. Push bare wire end in styrofoam to dry. Remove wax paper and attach poinsettia to mound with icing.

For leaves, lay 4″ florist's wire on wax paper. Using tube 65, pipe a leaf directly over wire end. Dry.

3. Arrange flowers in vases. Pipe a large tube 32 star on wax paper, push upside-down bell into it. Dry. Line with clear plastic, fill with royal icing and arrange flowers and leaves in vase. Dry.

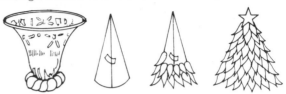

4. Make trees. Cover a Tree Former or cardboard cone with wax paper. Starting at base, pipe tube 74 leaves all around. Continue until cone is completely covered. Trees should be about $3\frac{7}{8}$″ high. Dry, then slip off cone. Add Color Flow star (see page 16) using pattern for smaller star on page 18. Attach with icing. Sprinkle trees with edible glitter.

DECORATE THE CAKE

1. Bake the cake tiers. You will need a two-layer 14″ square for the base, a two-layer 10″ square and a top tier 6″ square, 3″ high. Fill and ice all tiers with buttercream. Place the base tier on ruffle-trimmed board. Gently press 12″ round separator plate onto top surface to form guide for seven supporting dowel rods. Remove plate and push dowel rods to base, lift, clip and push back level with top of tier. Attach pegs to base of separator plate and push into position. Set 10″ tier on 11″ square separator plate and mark top with 7″ plate. Insert four dowel rods into tier as before and set 7″ plate with pegs on top of tier. Set 6″ tier on 7″ plate. Assemble tiers with pillars.

2. Decorate the base tier. First edge separator plate with tube 14 and trim with tube 3 string. Make a shield-shaped paper pattern to frame Angelinos. Transfer with toothpick and outline with tube 14, using an "i" motion. Attach Angelinos with mounds of icing. Pipe tube 22 star border at base. Use same tube for top shell border.

3. Decorate the middle tier. Edge separator plate the same as that on base tier. Pipe tube 20 upright shells at base. Drop curved guidelines on top and sides of tier with tube 2. Cover with tube 3 garland using up-and-down motion. Drop tube 2 string above, on and below side garlands. Pipe tube 2 bows on sides of cake. Trim upright shells at base with tube 2 string.

4. Decorate the top tier. Edge base with tube 20 stars and trim with tube 3 string. Trim top and sides of cake with garlands and string same as 12″ tier.

5. Set trees on plastic plates, securing with icing. Place between tiers. Arrange poinsettias in three Flower Spikes and push spikes into top tier. Glue Bridal Couple to plate and set in front of flowers. Attach vases to base plate on base tier with icing. Serves one hundred sixty guests.

Christmas Cakes *just for* Children

JACK FROST IN A STOCKING CAP

One of the joys of the Christmas season is creating special treats for the children. Here's a brand-new cake, sure to bring smiles of delight. It's Jack Frost himself, ready for a holiday party.

You will need one Ball Cake pan, one small Wonder Mold, the 5″ pan from round Mini-Tier set. A 10″ foil-covered cardboard circle, clean sponge, wax paper, soda straws, eight or ten jellybeans, a 1″ x 1″ piece of marzipan, food coloring, decorating tubes 16, 32 and 789, decorating bags, and butter—cream icing.

1. Make carrot nose. Prepare marzipan (recipe on page 52) and cut off 1″ piece. Tint it orange and shape into small carrot for nose.

2. Bake cakes. Bake one cake in Ball Pan, one in small Wonder Mold, and one in the 5″ round pan.

3. Ice and decorate cakes. Place round cake on foil-covered board and ice with Cake Icer tube 789. To make scarf ends, pipe tube 789 strips on curved surface and freeze until firm. Place iced ball cake on top of round cake, inserting a soda straw through both to hold them steady. Pat ball cake with sponge for stucco effect. Place Wonder Mold cake on top of ball, tilted to one side. Insert straws to hold it securely, one at an angle and one straight down through ball.

4. Decorate cap. Start at top, piping tube 16 red lines with zigzag motion. Repeat with blue icing and slightly longer strokes, then a row of red zigzag lines. Finish brim of cap with green tube 32 zigzags. For pompom, attach a large marshmallow with a toothpick and cover it with many green tube 16 spikes. Attach carrot nose with toothpick and position jellybeans for mouth and eyes. Put frozen scarf ends in position. Serves eighteen.

CANDY CANES!

The children's eyes will sparkle when they see these festive candy cane cakes brightening the holiday table. They're perfect for a party—easy to make.

You need a 6″ x 2″ round pan and an 8″ x 2″ square pan. Or the canes can be cut from a 9″ x 13″ sheet cake, using the pattern on page 33. You will also need decorating tube 13, food coloring and one recipe of buttercream icing. To make cutting easier, chill the cake first, then use a sharp knife.

1. Bake and cut cakes. Remove a 1½″ circle from the middle of round cake and cut this doughnut shape in half to make the "handles". Cut two pieces 2¼″ x 8″ and two wedges from square cake to complete the canes. Assemble, making canes face in opposite directions.

2. Ice smoothly. Then mark stripe pattern on cake bringing stripes down sides diagonally. With tube 13 pipe red stars over pattern lines. Pipe bottom border with same tube, red within the pattern lines and white stars to fill in. Each candy cane serves eight delighted children.

A MERRIMENT OF ELVES

HERE'S A HAPPY WAY to welcome returning carolers or brighten a children's party during the holidays. Bring out a merry crew of elves, their hats personalized with the guests' names. Make them with spice cake mix and serve with piping-hot cocoa for a treat on a frosty day.

To make these jolly elves, you need a set of small Wonder Mold cake pans, food coloring, stiff paper for hats, a little cornstarch, and for eight elves, three cups of buttercream icing. You also need tubes 2, 8, 10, 12, 13 and 18. One cake mix makes eight.

1. Bake cakes in small Wonder Molds, four to a pan. Cool and place on cardboard circles covered with foil. Ice smoothly with flesh-color icing made by adding one drop of copper color to four tablespoons white buttercream.

2. Decorate faces. Pipe features, using tube 2 for mouth and eyebrows, tube 12 for cheeks, tube 10 for nose and eyes. Pat cheeks, nose and eyes to flatten them, using tip of finger dipped in cornstarch. For ears, pipe a large tube 8 bulb and in front of that, pipe a C with tube 8.

3. Pipe hair with tube 2 lines on each head. It's fun to give each elf a different hair style. For curly hair, use a continuous circling motion.

4. Make hats. Cut 3″ circles of stiff paper and trim about ⅓ of each circle. Form a cone shape, adjust to fit elf's head, and tape. Set hat on head and trim with tube 13 zigzag border. Pipe a large tube 18 star at peak of hat and pull out many tube 13 stars to cover it and make a pompom. Pipe tube 1 name.

HELLO SANTA!

Bring forth a plate of smiling Santas to greet the family at Christmas brunch, or delight the children at a holiday party. Santas are fun to decorate, and easy, too.

You'll need Heart Cupcake Pans, decorating tubes 2, 8, 10, 12, 13 and 16, food coloring, decorating bags, about four cups buttercream icing, cornstarch, and a few toothpicks.

1. Bake cupcakes in Heart Cupcake Pans. (One mix makes eighteen.) When cool, ice tops with flesh-color icing, made by adding a very small amount of liquid copper food coloring on the tip of a toothpick to a little white icing.

2. Outline edge of hat with toothpick. Cover crown of hat with tube 13 stars and pipe tube 16 zigzags for cuff. To make pompom on hat, pipe one tube 18 star and cover with many tube 13 stars.

3. Make features, coloring small amounts of icing. Figure-pipe blue eyes with tube 8, deep pink cheeks with tube 12, red nose with tube 10 and mouth with tube 2. To flatten balls of icing for feaures, tap each ball lightly with finger dusted with cornstarch.

4. Add hair. Pipe c-motion swirls with tube 16 to make Santa's hair, beard and mustache.

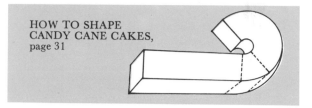

HOW TO SHAPE
CANDY CANE CAKES,
page 31

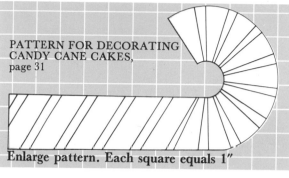

PATTERN FOR DECORATING
CANDY CANE CAKES,
page 31

Enlarge pattern. Each square equals 1″

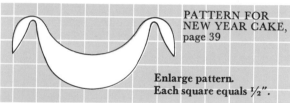

PATTERN FOR
NEW YEAR CAKE,
page 39

Enlarge pattern.
Each square equals ½″.

33

LIGHT THE CHRISTMAS CANDLES

Bake a candle centerpiece to give sparkle to your holiday table. Bedecked with holly, ribbon and brightly colored candles made of cake, it's a dessert to delight your guests.

For this cake you need three empty straight-sided cans: 5″ x 2¾″ diameter (15½ ounce vegetable can), 4″ x 2½″ diameter (10¾ ounce condensed soup can), and 3″ x 3″ diameter (15 ounce bean or mandarin orange can). You also need an 8″ x 2″ round pan for the base cake, heavy cardboard, decorating tubes 5, 6, 9, and 113, wax paper, dowel rods, ribbon, one cup marshmallow fluff (or boiled icing), four cups buttercream icing and food coloring.

1. Bake cakes, using your favorite pound cake recipe. Cakes baked in cans tend to mound up, which is desirable. Remove from pans. When cool, push a dowel rod about 2¾″ longer than cake, through each can cake. Cut a cardboard circle the diameter of each can cake and punch hole in center. Slip dowel rod through cake and circle. Freeze.

2. Pipe holly leaves. Cover a curved surface with wax paper and pipe holly leaves with tube 113. Pull out points with a damp brush. Freeze.

3. Ice cakes. Smoothly ice base cake. Place on 10″ foil-covered cardboard circle. Pipe bottom bulb border with tube 9. Ice sides of candle cakes.

34

4. Assemble. Position candles on base cake and push in dowel rods to cake board. Mound marshmallow fluff or boiled icing on top. Tint some icing orange and stripe inside of decorating bag with a spatula, then fill with yellow. Pipe four tube 6 flames around dowel rods. Position holly leaves, using dots of icing. Pipe tube 5 berries. Add a fluffy ribbon bow.

5. To serve, remove candles and dowel rods from cake and slice. Serves about twenty-two.

BAKE A TRAY OF TOYS

Here's a delightful way to spend a December afternoon—bake miniature cakes in the shape of toys. Decorate them in gay holiday colors, for a gift that's sure to please any child.

To make all three you need Mini-Toy cake pans, decorating tubes 1, 2, 4, 7, 13, 46, 102 and 103, six cups buttercream icing, decorating bags, food coloring, wax paper, a little cornstarch, and a mint patty to make the driver's face.

1. Bake cakes in Mini-Toy pans. Each pan takes one-fourth of a standard cake mix. Use the extra batter for cupcakes or to bake another toy. Cool, and coat with thinned buttercream icing.

2. To decorate doll, pipe tube 7 eyes, nose and mouth and flatten with finger dipped in cornstarch. Fill face and hands with tube 13 stars. Starting at feet, fill in boots and stockings with tube 13 stars and top stockings with tube 102 green ruffle. Next pipe tube 46 white straps for apron, holding tube serrated side down. Pipe tube 13 green trim on apron and fill in with white tube 13 stars. Finish dress with tube 13 red stars and tube 103 white ruffles. Pipe ruffles before stars on sleeves and after stars on neck and apron.

Pipe tube 2 hair, using circular motion for curls. Add tube 4 bows in hair, tube 1 bows on boots.

3. For the car, glaze windows and headlight with thinned buttercream icing. Pipe tube 4 steering wheel and outline window and headlight with tube 4. Secure mint patty in window with dot of icing and pipe tube 2 features and hair. Pipe tube 4 spokes and hub caps, and outline door and windows with tube 2. Now fill in entire car with tube 13 stars, changing colors of icing as picture indicates. Pipe tube 2 door handle. Overpipe all tube 2 and tube 4 lines.

4. To make teddy bear, outline eyes and nose with tube 2 and flow in thinned buttercream icing. Outline arms, legs and other features with tube 2 and fill in entire body with tube 13 stars. Each toy serves three.

Santa Express

MAKE THEM WITH CAKE, and cookie dough, and icing, and lots of love! These enchanting, edible gifts will delight your children. Perhaps they symbolize the actual gifts a child will receive, or they might serve as a party centerpiece and dessert. Each one is fun to make and to eat.

EVERYBODY WANTS A PUPPY!

For the youngsters who love a faithful family pet, or the boy who longs for his own puppy and is getting it this year, here's an ideal cake.

To make it you'll need the Lovable Animal Pan, decorating tubes 3, 7, 13, 14 and 15, decorating bags, food coloring and six cups buttercream icing. Make holly leaves as described on page 34.

1. Bake cake in Lovable Animal Pan, and cover with a thin coat of buttercream icing to seal crumbs.

2. Decorate cake. Pipe tube 7 eyes and nose, and flatten them slightly with finger dipped in cornstarch. Pipe tube 3 mouth, tube 13 stars for ear. To make features stand out, pipe muzzle, feet and tail with tube 14 elongated shells. Now cover body with tube 14 swirls, using a half-circular motion. Pipe tube 15 collar and add holly leaves and some red berries. When icing has dried, brighten eyes by brushing with corn syrup. Serves twelve.

A BALL TO PLAY WITH

Here's a colorful cake that's fun to create and so easy a child can help to decorate it. Make it in Christmas red and green.

You'll need a 6" Ball Shaped Pan, tube 16, two cups buttercream icing, food coloring, and string.

1. Bake cake in ball pan, cool and cover with thin coat of buttercream icing. Divide cake into sixths and mark off areas. Take a piece of string, measure circumference of ball and fold this piece into sixths. Using this, mark circumference in sixths. Now start at one of these marks and run string up to top of ball, and across to mark on opposite side. Go on down around ball to return to starting point. Allow string to mark icing. Repeat to divide into six areas.

2. Decorate cake. Divide icing into two parts, tint one red and one green. Fill in alternate segments of ball with tube 16 stars in red and green. Serves twelve.

PRESENTS ARE COMING BY THE TRUCKLOAD!

Here comes the Santa Express, loaded with goodies for youngsters of every age. Best of all, it's delicious! The truck body and gifts are cake, the trim is icing and crisp cookies.

You'll need 6" square cake pans, Little Loafer pans, four cups buttercream icing, two cups confectioners' sugar and two tablespoons of milk for glaze, decorat-

ing tubes 1, 13, 16, 44 and 102, decorating bags and food coloring. You also need a sharp knife, aluminum foil, and a clean, empty #2½ size can.

1. Bake three 6" x 6" cakes, each two layers. Trim one to 4" x 6" size. Bake four Little Loafer cakes, and cut one in half to make smaller packages.

2. Make one recipe Roll-out Cookie Dough (page 12), roll out to ⅛" thickness. Cut out two 3¼" x 3" side windows, one 5¼" x 3" front window, one 6½" x 4½" cab top, one 6½" x ½" bumper, one 2½" x ½" grill top, four 2¼" wheels, five strips 4½" x ¾" for fenders and sign, three 1¼" circles for driver's head and headlights. Bake the four fenders on empty can covered with aluminum foil, crumpled up at edges to keep them from sliding off. Bake other cookies flat.

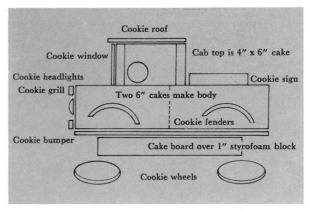

3. Ice and decorate cookies. Mix two cups confectioners' sugar with milk, a tablespoon at a time, and tint. Use this mixture to glaze all the cookie pieces. Decorate driver's head with tube 1. Pipe tube 13 spokes and rim on wheels, tube 1 beading on headlights and tube 1 lettering on sign.

4. Cover cakes with thinned buttercream and assemble, following diagram. Set truck on 6" x 12" cake board, then on 9" x 4" x 1" block of styrofoam. Attach windows, roof and driver's head with dots of icing. Outline door with tube 1. Pipe tube 16 stars to cover rest of truck. Ice Little Loafer cakes and trim with tube 44 ribbons. Pipe tube 102 bows separately on wax paper and freeze.

5. Pipe tube 16 strips down front of truck. Attach the rest of the cookie pieces with dots of icing. Pipe door handle and overpipe door outline with tube 1. Place packages in truck and attach bows with dots of icing. Serves twenty.

CANDLE TREES ALL AGLOW

Let's make a party sparkle by serving these charming Candle Tree Cakes. Cut from a single large loaf cake, they're easy to make and decorate.

You'll need four cups buttercream, ⅛ cup Color Flow icing, decorating tubes 2, 4, 9, 16 and 73, decorating bags, wax paper, cardboard, food coloring, tree pattern (page 18) and Long Loaf pan.

1. Make four Color Flow stars. Tape pattern on page 18 to cardboard and cover with wax paper. Outline with tube 1 and flow in color. Dry overnight.

2. Bake cake in Long Loaf pan, cool, and cut in two. Ice both halves with buttercream icing and place upright on serving plate.

3. Decorate cakes. Place tree pattern against cakes and trace with toothpick. Starting at top, pipe three tube 16 lines for trunk, one line on each side of cake and one down the middle, at the corner.

Pipe tube 16 branches at an angle to the trunk. Pipe tube 73 leaves, making those on the branches lie flat and those on the trunk stand out at an angle. Pipe tube 9 bulb border around base of both cakes. To make tiny candles, pipe a tube 4 line topped with a tube 2 "flame". Attach stars with dots of icing. The two cakes serve sixteen.

DANCING THE NEW YEAR IN

Gay and carefree, that's the mood of this New Year's cake. Festooned with ribbons of icing and golden bells, it's a delightful dessert for a New Year's party or open house.

You'll need four cups buttercream icing, two tablespoons royal icing, food coloring, piping gel, decorating tubes 1s, 1, 17, 19, 103 and 104, and decorating bags. You also need a pattern for the banner (page 33), small knife, mint sugar (recipe page 60), hard candy (recipe page 11), hard candy Bell Molds, and the Dancing Cherub figure.

1. Make banner of mint sugar. Roll out tinted mint sugar, lay pattern on it and cut it out with sharp knife. Work quickly as it dries fast. With tube 1s and royal icing, pipe on lettering.

2. Make hard candy and pour into Bell Molds. Cool and harden in refrigerator about 15 minutes. Pop out. You'll need eighteen bells, mold holds twenty.

3. Bake cake. Bake two layers in 10″ round cake pans, fill and ice with buttercream.

4. Decorate cake. For decorating, make buttercream icing a little stiffer by adding confectioners' sugar, a tablespoon or two at a time. Pipe tube 19 shell border around base of cake, and just above that drop a row of tube 104 swags, topping each with a tube 17 star. Now fold a 10″ circle of paper into twelfths, cut scallops, and placing this pattern on cake top, trace scallops with pin or toothpick. Over these lines, pipe tube 103 swags, topping each with a tube 17 star. Pipe tube 17 shell border around top of cake.

5. Attach bells to side of cake in pairs, using dots of icing, and pipe bows above them with tube 1 and piping gel. Place Dancing Cherub in center of cake top, banner draped across his hands and secured with glue. Pipe small mounds of icing around base and set bells in place. Serves fourteen.

CHRISTMAS WOULDN'T BE CHRISTMAS without candy! Old time favorites like fudge, cherry divinity, chocolate truffles, Turkish delight. Luxurious chocolates a pastry chef would be proud to create. Dainty fondant bonbons in pastel colors. Make your own candy this year—pack it for gifts, serve it to guests, treat the children. Everyone will love these special sweets, and you'll enjoy the compliments creative candy-making brings.

LET'S MAKE GIANT LOLLIPOPS!

Arrange them like fresh flowers in a centerpiece, or hand them out to the children as a special holiday treat. Christmas Lollipops will be a popular addition to your repertoire of holiday goodies.

To make them, you need aluminum foil cut in 12" squares, vegetable oil, a deep, straight-sided 2½ or 3-quart saucepan, a pastry brush, candy thermometer, cookie sheets, Really Big Cookie Cutters or your own favorite cutters in 4½" to 6" size, lollipop sticks (made for taffy apples or popsicles) or ⅛" wooden dowel rods, plus candy ingredients. To trim the lollipops, you'll need decorating tube 1, a decorating bag and ribbon. One cup royal icing trims nine or more.

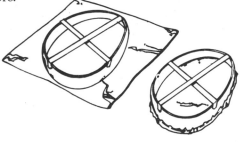

1. Make hard candy syrup, using recipe on page 11. Add food color at beginning of cooking process. This makes three giant lollipops. Make one batch at a time, as syrup may solidify too fast if you mix a larger amount. Be sure to include flavoring.

2. Prepare cutters while candy cooks. Oil the inside of each cutter, and set it in the middle of a 12" square of foil. Crumple foil around the outside of the cutter, keeping the part inside the cutter smooth and flat. Place cutters on a cookie sheet.

3. When thermometer in candy reaches 280°, turn heat to low, or candy will burn. At this point stir in flavoring. When candy reaches 300°, pour it into cutters, to a depth of about ⅜". Let cool, then place in freezer about ten minutes to harden. Repeat steps 1, 2, and 3 until you have made as many lollipops as you wish.

4. Remove cutters and add sticks. Take lollipops out of freezer and remove cutters, then peel off foil. To attach stick, dip one end into a batch of clear Hard Candy Syrup (basic recipe without color or flavor added). Place stick on lollipop and brush on more syrup. They'll be dry enough to handle in about ten minutes. Pipe free-hand trim with tube 1 and royal icing. Tie on ribbon bows. Keep away from sunlight or direct heat. To store Christmas Lollipops, pack them flat in a cool, dry place.

MAKE LITTLE LOLLIPOPS TOO! Make them just as you did the jewel ornaments, using the Stars and Shapes hard candy molds. Attach sticks as described above. One recipe makes sixteen.

Candy for Christmas

THE JOY OF MAKING CHRISTMAS CANDIES

Christmas is a time of delight for those who love sweets, and some of the best loved candies are easiest to make. So plan a candy-making party for the family or a few close friends.

Teen-agers and smaller children, too, will have fun helping make such old favorites as divinity, fudge, truffles, Turkish Delight and candied lemon and orange peel coated with chocolate.

TWO TONE FUDGE

This easy recipe calls for a double batch of fudge, for double enjoyment.

⅔ cup milk or cream
2 cups sugar
2 ounces (2 squares) unsweetened
  chocolate, chopped
2 tablespoons light corn syrup
2 tablespoons butter
few grains salt
1 teaspoon vanilla extract
1 cup coarsely chopped walnuts

1. Combine milk, sugar, chocolate, corn syrup and butter in a three-quart saucepan and heat slowly, stirring until sugar dissolves. Wash down sugar crystals with wet pastry brush. Cook, stirring occasionally, until temperature reaches soft-ball stage, 236°.

2. Add salt and vanilla extract. Cool mixture, without stirring, to lukewarm (about 120°).

3. Add chopped nuts and beat until mixture becomes creamy and starts to lose its shine. Pour into buttered 8″ x 8″ x 2″ pan. (Note: if mixture becomes too stiff to pour add a little cream.)

4. Now prepare another complete batch of fudge using ingredients listed above, except omit the chocolate and nuts. Beat White Fudge until creamy, spread over chocolate fudge in the pan. Cool and cut into squares. Makes about 2½ pounds.

CHERRY PECAN DIVINITY*

Light as air and tart-sweet as fresh cherries, this is the perfect candy to nibble between those rich holiday meals. Easy to make, too!

3 cups sugar
¾ cup light corn syrup
¾ cup water
2 egg whites
1 package (3 ounces) cherry-flavored gelatin
1 cup chopped pecans

1. Combine sugar, corn syrup and water in heavy two-quart saucepan. Cook over medium heat, stirring until sugar dissolves. Bring to boiling, set candy thermometer in place and cook to hard-ball stage

*Thanks to Mrs. Richard Kelly, Brandonville, W. Va.,
  for basic recipe.

(approximately 252°).

2. Meanwhile, beat egg whites with electric mixer until stiff, but not dry, peaks form. Beat in gelatin.

3. When syrup reaches 252°, pour in a thin stream over egg whites, beating constantly. Beat as long as possible. Use wooden spoon if too stiff for mixer. Add nuts. Turn into buttered 9″ square pan.

4. Cool until firm. Cut into squares. Makes about two pounds of divinity.

CHOCOLATE TRUFFLES

Here's a confection that truly melts in your mouth! A luscious blending of chocolate and coffee flavors, it's sure to please your holiday guests.

2 tablespoons double-strength coffee
½ pound semi-sweet chocolate, melted
¼ cup heavy cream, scalded
2 egg yolks, slightly beaten
¼ cup butter
1 teaspoon vanilla extract
½ cup confectioners' sugar
finely chopped walnuts or pecans

1. Stir coffee into chocolate, set aside to cool.

2. Blend hot cream into egg yolks. Immediately pour into small heavy saucepan or small double boiler. Cook, stirring constantly, three to five minutes or until mixture thickens. Cool.

3. Cream butter with vanilla extract and confectioners' sugar. Gradually add cooled chocolate and egg mixtures, and mix well.

4. Place bowl over ice and water. Continue to mix until firm enough to shape into thirty-six 1″ balls. Keep mixture over ice and water while shaping them.

5. Roll each ball in chopped nuts. Place on wax paper lined tray and chill. Makes one pound.

RASPBERRY TURKISH DELIGHT

Designed for those who like sweets with a tang.

2 tablespoons (2 envelopes) unflavored gelatin
½ cup puréed thawed frozen raspberries
1 tablespoon lemon juice
2 cups sugar
¼ teaspoon salt
⅔ cup water
food coloring

1. Sprinkle dry gelatin over a mixture of thawed raspberry purée and lemon juice.

2. Combine sugar, salt, and water in a heavy saucepan. Stir over low heat until sugar is dissolved. Cover tightly and cook over medium heat until mixture comes to boiling. Boil two minutes. Uncover, put candy thermometer in place and continue cooking to 236° without stirring.

3. Remove from heat. Add gelatin mixture and food coloring, then return to heat and cook to 224° while stirring constantly.

4. Pour into a lightly buttered 9″ x 5″ loaf pan to depth of ½″. Let stand till firm or overnight.

5. Sprinkle top of jelly with sifted confectioners' sugar. Using spatula coated with sugar, loosen jelly from pan. Invert onto board lightly dusted with confectioners' sugar. Cut into rectangles, using knife coated with sugar. Dust pieces with more confectioners' sugar. Makes about 1¾ pounds.

CHOCOLATE COVERED PEEL

3 large thick-skinned oranges or
   2 large thick-skinned lemons
¹⁄₁₆ teaspoon salt
1 cup granulated sugar
2 tablespoons honey or light corn syrup
½ cup water
1 pound tempered milk or dark chocolate

1. Wash fruit. Cut into lengthwise quarters, through skins only. Pull off skins and put into saucepan.

2. Add cold water to a depth of 2″, then add salt and bring to boiling. Boil gently ten minutes or more or until peel is tender. Drain. Pour cold water over peel. Cut peel into ¼″ strips.

3. Make a syrup of sugar, honey and water in a 1-quart saucepan. Boil, uncovered, to very soft ball stage, 230° to 234°.

4. Add peel, pushing it under the syrup. Boil gently, uncovered, at 220° for fifteen minutes or more, or until peel becomes translucent.

5. When peel is done, lift from syrup with tongs and place on rack over wax paper covered tray. Let stand an hour or more, until peel is cold and surface has dried. Keep pieces in a single layer.

6. To chocolate-coat peel, let it stand long enough to form crust. Then put each strip on fork or hold with tongs and dip into tempered chocolate. Directions for tempering chocolate are on page 45. Cool strips until set. Makes about one pound.

At left: Candied Orange and Lemon Peel, chocolate-coated. At top: Raspberry Turkish Delight and Two-Tone Fudge. At right: Cherry Pecan Divinity and Chocolate Truffles.

Candies with a Continental Flair

YES, YOU CAN MAKE these luxurious chocolates! Master pastry chef Larry Olkiewicz shares his own recipes for European candies unobtainable in even the most expensive shops in the United States.

Fondant is an ingredient in several of the candies, and for chocolates as fine as these, the refined flavor of homemade fondant is essential. So study the fondant method on page 48 and prepare a batch. Marzipan is also used for some of the candies—you'll find a good recipe on page 52.

Making these chocolates is a time-taking, but very rewarding, task, so shop carefully for top-quality ingredients. Chef Olkiewicz recommends using Swiss chocolate, usually obtainable from candy shops or the import section of grocery stores.

All the recipes except for Mozartkugeln yield about one hundred candies. We recommend you plan to make two varieties so you will have both dark and milk chocolate ready for contrasting trims.

Almost all of these candies have brandy or other liqueur as an ingredient. This, of course, adds delicious flavor and perfume, and also serves as a preservative so that the candies can be stored in a cool dark place for a long time.

Here is some advice from Chef Olkiewicz to guide you in your candy-making adventure:

1. All chocolate must be tempered before using for decorating or dipping. Here is the way to temper chocolate: heat water to about 175° in the bottom of a 1½ quart double boiler. Remove from heat and place cut-up chocolate (one cup at a time), in the top half of double boiler to melt. Stir chocolate every ten minutes until melted and at a temperature of 110°. Remove melted chocolate from heat and cool until almost stiff. Then it is ready to heat for dipping or decorating.

2. You will need to melt the tempered chocolate before dipping or decorating. Milk and dark chocolate are melted to different temperatures. **To melt milk chocolate** reheat over hot water until candy thermometer registers between 86° and 88°. **To melt dark chocolate** reheat over hot water to between 90° and 92°. Remove chocolate from hot water while there are still a few unmelted lumps.

3. To fill molds with chocolate, put the melted chocolate into a parchment paper cone you roll yourself and cut the tip. Fill molds. Tap mold lightly after filling to make sure all indentations are filled. Set the molds in the refrigerator for ten or fifteen minutes until hard. Invert molds to drop out forms. Any unused chocolate can be re-melted to use again.

4. To pipe trims put a small amount of melted chocolate into a parchment paper cone with cut tip.

5. Any liqueur left over after marinating fruits for candies can be put to good use. Use it to flavor dessert sauces, puddings or fruit compotes.

6. The only special pieces of equipment needed for these candies are plastic candy molds, a candy thermometer and a bent fork for dipping.

CHOCOLATE LADY FINGERS

This is a favorite continental sweet. Simply melt dark or milk chocolate, pour into lady finger candy molds, refrigerate ten minutes to harden and unmold. Trim with scrolls and dots of contrasting chocolate. If you do not have lady finger molds, use any chocolate mold and trim with contrasting chocolate. One pound of chocolate makes about thirty candies.

VODKAKIRSCHEN
Vodka Cherries

100 maraschino cherries, stems on
Vodka to cover cherries, about 2 cups
4 pounds milk chocolate
5 cups Wilton fondant
Start two months before the holidays to make these luscious candies—they're worth the planning.

1. Drain the cherries well. Put in jar, cover with vodka and cover tightly. Allow to marinate eight weeks or more.
2. When you are ready to make the candy, drain the cherries well and put on paper towels for about half an hour to dry. Warm the fondant to almost 100°, or dipping consistency. Holding cherry by stem, or on dipping fork, dip each into the fondant and set on wax paper to harden, about half an hour.
3. Melt the chocolate and dip each cherry to just about one-third its height. (This provides a firm base for the candies.) Harden in refrigerator about ten minutes. Now dip each candy completely in chocolate, letting the chocolate cover about ¼″ of the stem to provide a firm seal. Harden again in refrigerator for about ten minutes, then decorate with leaf shapes. Cut tip of paper cone in a downward-facing V-shape for leaves.
4. Store in a cool, dark place for a week to ten days for fondant to liquefy and turn into a delicious syrup. **Recipe makes one hundred candies.**

APRIKOSENSTUECKCHEN
Apricot Triangles

4½ ounces finely-chopped dried apricots
6 ounces peach brandy
12 ounces almond paste
3 ounces confectioners' sugar
4 pounds dark chocolate
pistachio slivers for garnish

1. Soak the apricots in the peach brandy in a tightly covered jar for two days or more. Mix the almond paste with the sugar, kneading with hands. Pour the marinated apricots into a sieve to drain. Do not press out brandy. Add apricots to almond paste mixture and knead to a soft paste.
2. Dust work surface with confectioners' sugar and roll out paste to ⅜″ thickness. Cut into ¾″ triangles. Let the triangles dry about one hour.
3. Now dip the triangles into melted chocolate with a fork. After the second candy has been dipped, go back to the first and mark a criss-cross design on the top with the fork. Continue in this way until all have been dipped and marked. Garnish each with a sliver of pistachio. Makes one hundred candies.

Pictured above, clockwise, starting at top center: Chocolate Lady Fingers, Vodkakirschen, Aprikosenstueckchen, Kurpflaumen, Koenigsbergermarzipan, Canacherollon, and in the center, Honigbonbon.

KURPFLAUMEN
Royal Chocolate Prunes

100 small pitted prunes
½ cup brandy
1 cup marzipan (⅓ of the recipe on page 52)
4 pounds dark chocolate

1. Put the prunes in a bowl, sprinkle with brandy and let sit about half an hour. Drain prunes in a sieve and transfer to dry on paper towels.
2. Mix the marzipan with the brandy poured off the prunes. (You may need to add a little more brandy to form a soft paste.) Form this mixture into ovals the size and shape of a prune pit. Force these "pits" into the prunes.
3. Dip into melted chocolate, dry on wax paper and pipe the little "shoelace" design on top of each candy. This makes one hundred Royal Prunes.

KOENIGSBERGERMARZIPAN
Flamed Marzipan

Decorative toasted confections with a nutty flavor.
   2 pounds marzipan (1⅓ of the recipe on page 52)
   2 teaspoons rosewater (available in pharmacies or grocery stores)
   1 pound dark chocolate

1. Mix the marzipan with the rosewater, kneading well. Form into twists, spirals or curves. Let dry overnight.
2. Run the marzipan under the broiler until golden. Watch carefully as marzipan burns easily.
3. When cool, dip in melted chocolate, covering base of marzipan only. Dry on wax paper. Recipe makes one hundred candies.

CANACHEROLLEN
Chocolate Drums

8 ounces marzipan (⅓ of recipe on page 52)
Chocolate Canache (recipe below)
4 pounds milk chocolate

1. Roll the marzipan in a rectangular shape ⅛" thick. Spread with the canache and roll up like a jelly roll to form a 1" diameter cylinder. You will have two or three of these cylinders. Wrap in wax paper and harden in refrigerator for about an hour.
2. Cut in 1" slices, dip in melted chocolate and dry on wax paper. Decorate with dark chocolate. Yield is one hundred chocolates.

Chocolate Canache
1 cup dark chocolate, tempered and melted
⅓ cup heavy cream
1½ tablespoons confectioners' sugar

Mix all ingredients with a wooden spatula. Place in refrigerator until almost set, then use immediately.

HONIGBONBON
Honey Fruit Bars

   12 ounces almond paste
   2 tablespoons brandy
   1 tablespoon honey
   3 ounces finely chopped dates
   3 ounces finely chopped dried figs
   4 pounds milk chocolate

1. Soften the almond paste by kneading in the honey and brandy. Knead in the chopped fruit and roll out to ½" thickness on surface dusted with confectioners' sugar. Cut into circles with a ¾" diameter cutter.
2. Dip in melted chocolate and dry on wax paper. Decorate with buttons and dots of chocolate. This makes one hundred candies.

MOZARTKUGELN

This delicious confection is a specialty of Salzburg. There it is wrapped in gold foil bearing a portrait of Mozart, that city's most illustrious citizen.
   8 ounces of marzipan (⅓ of the recipe on page 52)
   4 ounces finely-chopped pistachios
   2½-ounce bar of nougat (purchase in import candy section of grocery store)
   2 pounds dark chocolate

1. Knead together the marzipan and chopped pistachio. Roll out on board dusted with confectioners' sugar to ⅛" thickness. Cut into circles about 1½" in diameter with a cookie cutter.
2. Pinch off pieces of the nougat and form into small balls. Put a ball on each marzipan circle and wrap the nougat, drawing edges of marzipan together.
3. Dip each wrapped ball in chocolate, keeping seam side at bottom. Dry on wax paper. Lacking Mozart's portrait, decorate with a spiral of milk chocolate, piped with a paper cone. The yield is fifty delicious Mozartkugeln.

MARZIPAN OVALS

16 ounces marzipan (⅔ of the recipe on page 52)
1 ounce cherry brandy
Additional brandy for brushing
4 ounces English black currant jam (or other top quality, heavy jam)
4 pounds milk chocolate

1. Knead the cherry brandy into the marzipan. Roll out on board dusted with confectioners' sugar to ½" thickness. Cut with oval cutter about 1½" x 1".

2. Cut a hole in each oval with base of any decorating tube. Combine cut-out circles and roll as thinly as possible. Cut into ovals with same oval cutter, brush with brandy and set cut-out ovals on top.

3. Fill the centers with the jam, using a paper cone. Dip in chocolate with a fork, keeping the top up. Dry on wax paper. Pipe design on top. Recipe makes one hundred ovals.

EGGNOG CUPS

These candies may be molded in foil cups, or more conveniently, in the plastic Flute Candy Mold.

    4 pounds dark chocolate
    3½ ounces almond paste
    1 ounce corn syrup
    2 ounces sweetened condensed milk
    3 ounces Advokatt liqueur
    Milk chocolate for trim

1. Make the chocolate shells first. Melt the chocolate and pour into the molds. Turn molds over to tip out excess chocolate and let harden.

2. Gradually add the syrup to the almond paste, kneading until well mixed, then add the condensed milk and liqueur, mixing thoroughly with a spoon to a soft paste. Put the mixture in a paper cone, cut off the tip, and fill the chocolate shells just ¾ full. Set aside to harden a little for about ten minutes.

3. Melt the left-over chocolate, put into paper cone with cut tip, and cover the molds to the rim. Refrigerate five to ten minutes to harden, remove from molds. Decorate with zigzag line and dot of milk chocolate. Recipe makes one hundred chocolates.

NOUGATBLAETTER
Nougat Filled Leaves

    6 tablespoons Wilton fondant (see page 48)
    3 tablespoons finely-ground toasted hazelnuts
    3½ teaspoons instant coffee
    3 tablespoons brandy
    4 pounds dark chocolate

1. Warm the fondant and mix well with the hazelnuts, coffee and brandy.

2. Make chocolate shells using the oval leaf-imprinted plastic mold and the same method as directed in the recipe for Eggnog Cups. When the shells are dry, fill them with the fondant mixture ¾ full, using a paper cone. Warm the mixture if necessary for easier piping. Let stand for one hour, then cover the molds to the top with melted chocolate. Place in refrigerator ten minutes and unmold. Yield is one hundred leaves.

RUMROSINENHAEUFCHEN
Rum Raisin Mounds

Raisins never tasted so good!

    3 cups white raisins
    1½ cups rum
    3 pounds dark chocolate

1. Put the raisins in a jar, pour over the rum and soak, tightly covered, for three hours. Drain by putting raisins in a sieve, but not pressing out.

2. Fold raisins into melted chocolate, working quickly. Drop by teaspoon onto wax paper to dry. One hundred mounds.

STIFTELMANDELHAEUFCHEN
Butter Almonds

    3 cups slivered almonds (not sliced)
    3 tablespoons butter
    1 tablespoon vanilla sugar
    3 pounds milk chocolate

If vanilla sugar is not available, make your own by sprinkling one tablespoon confectioners' sugar with six drops of vanilla and mixing well. Or bury a vanilla bean in one cup of confectioners' sugar and store covered for a week or as long as you like. Use for icing or any dessert.

1. Melt the butter in a heavy frying pan, add the almonds, sprinkle with vanilla sugar and stir over low heat until almonds are golden. Use a wooden spatula. Cool.

2. Fold into the melted chocolate, working quickly. Drop by teaspoon into long "streamlined" shapes. Recipe yields one hundred.

On the tray above, left to right: Mozartkugeln, Marzipan Ovals, Nougatblaetter, Eggnog Cups, Rumrosinenhaeufchen and Stiftelmandelhaeufchen.

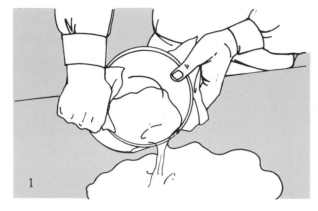

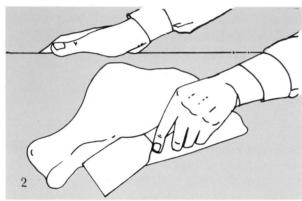

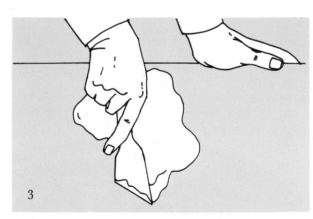

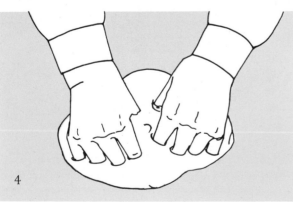

THE AGE-OLD ART
OF FONDANT CONFECTIONERY

Haven't you often admired the smooth, lustrous finish that professional chefs give to petits fours and wedding cakes? You can do it too—and create French bonbons and dainty mints as well—by mastering the easy art of fondant.

Fondant is such a simple substance that it seems almost a miracle that it can taste so delicious! So make a batch of fondant this holiday season. It's versatile, you can tint and flavor it to your taste, will keep well for weeks, and will certainly enhance your reputation as a master *patissiere*.

The only special tools you need are a marble slab, about 2' x 3' (a heat- and mar-proof plastic table will do), a candy scraper and a candy thermometer. Here Norman Wilton shows you the step-by-step way to perfect fondant. This recipe yields five pounds, but it may easily be doubled.

WILTON FONDANT RECIPE

3½ pounds granulated sugar
2 cups water
½ pound glucose (obtainable at bakery supply companies)

Combine all ingredients in a large, heavy saucepan and heat until all the sugar is dissolved. When syrup looks clear, wash down sides of pan with a brush dipped in warm water to remove sugar crystals. Repeat this procedure several times during cooking. Increase heat and boil until it reaches 240° on a candy thermometer. Remove from heat.

1. Immediately pour the mixture onto the slab or plastic table. As soon as it has slightly cooled (a touch of a finger will make the surface crinkle) start to move it with the scraper.

2. Working from the edges, push under the fondant and lift it up and over to the center. Keep the mass in constant motion, repeating the up-and-over motion. Work fast and with an even rhythm.

3. As you work, the fondant will become creamy and whiten. Keep working it with the scraper in the same rapid, even rhythm. In about four minutes, you will have formed a mound so stiff you can stand the scraper straight up in it. Cover the mound with a damp cloth, and let it stand for about five minutes.

4. Now knead the mound of fondant, just as you would bread dough. Very quickly it will soften and become creamy. You can take out a portion of it to use immediately for mints or icing or any other purpose. While using, keep covered with a damp cloth to prevent drying. Keep unused fondant well covered in an air-tight container. It will keep at room temperature for weeks—ready to be warmed for future projects.

HOMEMADE MINT PATTIES

Spectacular for a holiday party, but very easy to make. Put about a pound of fondant in the top of a double boiler and heat, stirring constantly, just until fondant becomes pourable. Too much heat and fondant will become dull and too thin. Add flavoring and liquid food coloring.

There are two ways to form the mints. The traditional way is with a mint patty funnel. Put the stick in the funnel so pointed end closes the opening and pour in warmed fondant. Use a length of fine-ribbed rubber matting, or just wax paper, to drop the mints on. Now lift the stick briefly so fondant runs out and forms a patty, then drop stick to close flow. Go along briskly, with an even rhythm.

Or you may pour the warmed fondant in a decorating bag fitted with tube 12 and drop the patties. Rhythm is important here too. Hold your finger over tube opening after each mint is formed.

When mints have set, decorate with tube 2 and royal icing. Make tiny "dot" flowers and leaves, holly sprigs (pull out points of leaves with small brush), and loving mistletoe. You will have created about three dozen tiny masterpieces.

DAINTY FRENCH BONBONS
EASY TO MAKE WITH FONDANT

Surprise everyone this Christmas with these delectable pastel bonbons! You'll be surprised, too, at how easy it is to make these impressive sweets.

You'll need about two pounds of fondant (see page 48), one recipe of marzipan (page 52) and about half a cup of royal icing for trim. Thin the icing with two teaspoons of light corn syrup for a glossy appearance. Have ready a double boiler, food coloring, a bent fork for dipping, wax paper and a decorating bag fitted with tube 3.

1. Make bonbon centers. Divide marzipan into thirds and knead one-fourth cup of any of the ingredients listed below into each portion. You may also knead in a drop or two of flavoring. Shape marzipan into long cylinders, cut off 1″ pieces and form into balls.

    chopped candied cherries or pineapple
    chopped dried apricots or peaches
    chopped dates or raisins
    finely chopped nuts
    coconut
    finely chopped candied orange or lemon peel
    mixed chopped candied fruit

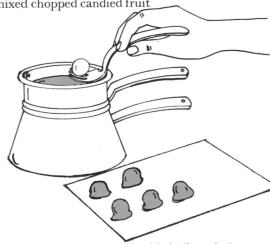

2. Warm the fondant in a double boiler, stirring constantly until it becomes just liquid enough to dip. Do not overheat, or it will lose its sheen. Remove from heat and add flavor and food coloring of your choice. Place a marzipan center on the bent fork and dip into the warmed fondant. Lift out and place on wax paper to set.

3. Decorate the candies with a swirl of tinted icing piped with tube 3. This makes about thirty bonbons.

CLASSIC PETITS FOURS IN HOLIDAY FONDANT DRESS

Give your holiday party a touch of elegance by serving these dainty petits fours. They'll impress your guests, especially when they discover you made them yourself, fondant coating and all.

For these party delicacies you'll need a double boiler, cookie cutters, sharp knife, wire rack, cookie sheet, spatula, tube 1, food colors and piping gel. You'll need three cups buttercream icing and two and a half pounds of fondant (page 48).

1. Bake a pound or sponge cake in a 12″ x 18″ x 1″ pan. Chill or freeze the cake, cut into dainty shapes with cookie cutters or a sharp knife. The cakes in the picture below are 2″ or less across.

2. Ice cakes with thinned buttercream icing to seal the crumbs and give a base for the fondant.

3. Warm the fondant in double boiler over medium heat, stirring constantly until it is of pourable consistency. Do not overheat, or it will become too thin and lose its characteristic shine. Fondant should be thick enough to cover cake, soft enough to pour and spread by itself. Set cakes on a wire rack placed in a cookie sheet. Pour fondant over them, touching up any bare spots with the spatula. Fondant that drips into cookie sheet may be used again. Let fondant set.

4. Add sparkling trims with tinted piping gel and tube 1. Use your imagination to create freehand designs that express the Christmas spirit. Makes about sixty beautiful petits fours.

MARZIPAN is easy and fun to work with, as chefs have known since the days of the ancient Persians. Once a closely guarded secret among skilled chefs and confectioners, marzipan is really simple to work with and has become a traditional Christmas treat. You'll enjoy mastering the art of modeling it into flowers, fruit, and figures. The resulting masterpieces can be used for cake trims, centerpieces, displays or gifts.

MARZIPAN RECIPE

1 cup almond paste (8 ounce can)
2 egg whites, unbeaten
3 cups confectioners' sugar
½ teaspoon vanilla or rum flavor

Knead almond paste by hand in a bowl. Add egg whites and mix well. Continue kneading as you add sugar, one cup at a time, and flavoring, until marzipan feels like heavy pie dough. Cover with plastic wrap, then place in tightly covered container in refrigerator where it will keep for months. This recipe makes thirty-nine pieces of fruit.

Marzipan can be tinted any color. Knead in liquid food coloring, one drop at a time, until you reach any shade you desire.

To add a blush of color, as on a peach, mix food color, one drop at a time, with a few drops of kirsch or any white liqueur. Dip small artists' brush into this liquid and brush lightly on piece to be tinted. Tint will dry in about five minutes.

To glaze marzipan pieces, combine ½ cup corn syrup and one cup water, heat to boiling and brush on with small artists' brush. This gives a soft shine. For a high gloss, use just one or two tablespoons water with ½ cup corn syrup.

To put marzipan pieces together, touch lightly with sponge soaked in egg white, then fix to second piece with turning motion.

All the tools you will need for marzipan work are an orange stick sharpened to a point at one end and a small kitchen knife with a sharp blade. To add glaze or tint, use a small artists' brush.

HOW TO FORM MARZIPAN FRUIT

Although the method is simple, modeling marzipan into realistic shapes does take practice. First dust

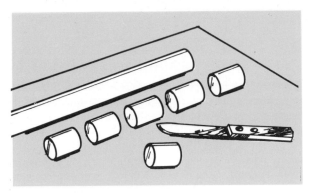

table lightly with confectioners' sugar, then with palms of hands, roll tinted marzipan into cylinders about 12¼" long and ⅞" in diameter. Cut into 1" pieces. This will assure a uniform size for all fruit.

All the fruit pictured here starts with a ball of marzipan. Roll the cut section between your palms until you achieve a nice ball shape. Then modify the ball for various fruits.

For apple, indent ends slightly, add clove stem. For orange, roll ball on grater to get rough skin, insert clove stem. For lemon, model oval shape with slightly pointed ends, roll on grater. Then brush green tint on tips. Make pears in modified teardrop shape, brush rosy tint on one side. For banana, roll slim, tapered shape and curve ends in slightly. Add touches of brown tint. For peach, form a groove on one side with orange stick, indent ends, and add a rosy tint on one side.

Once you get the hang of it, working with marzipan is fun. And it's so easy even the children can help you make attractive fruits and figures, cake trims and centerpieces.

HERE'S A PRETTY WAY to share your creative efforts with friends. Arrange a compote of marzipan fruits, and wrap them in sparkling clear plastic and holiday ribbon for Christmas giving. Add "orange blossoms" piped with tube 104 and white royal icing. Pipe tube 1 yellow dots at center.

Marzipan...
the Christmas Art

COLORFUL MARZIPAN FRUIT TREES

Display these gay little trees on the mantel or coffee table, or set one at each place for a festive, take-home gift. They're sure to win compliments!

Each tree takes ½ recipe of marzipan (see page 52). You'll also need liquid food coloring, decorating tubes 2, 5 and 67, decorating bags, one cup royal icing, Petite Heart Ornament Bases, a small brush, a grater, and whole cloves. Also, you will need ½ cup corn syrup, a few drops of kirsch or any white liqueur, and ribbon for trim.

1. Prepare marzipan. Divide to provide one-half batch for each tree. Tint each portion, kneading in liquid food color one drop at a time until natural color is achieved. Shape each portion into a long roll about ⅞″ in diameter.

2. Shape fruits. Cut each roll into 1″ pieces, and roll pieces into balls. You'll need nineteen fruits for each tree. Roll orange balls over grater, insert clove stems. For lemons, shape yellow balls into ovals with pointed ends, roll on grater. Model red balls into apples, and pipe tube 2 brown icing stems. Let dry 48 hours.

3. Apply tint and glaze. Brush tips of lemons with a tint of green, made from one drop green food color stirred into a few drops of kirsch. Let dry about 15 minutes. Then combine ½ cup corn syrup and 1 or 2 tablespoons water, heat to boiling and brush on fruits to glaze them. Let dry three to four hours.

4. Assemble trees. Pipe a tube 5 circle of royal icing around top of ornament base. Lay six fruits on the icing. Now put five fruits in position for next layer. Lift them off, pipe dots of icing where they touch the first layer, and set them in place. Repeat with a layer of four, then three, then one on top. Dry thoroughly. When all trees are assembled and dry, pipe tube 67 leaves between fruits. Pipe two tube 67 leaves at top of each tree. Trim with ribbon bows.

LIGHT UP YOUR TABLE WITH A POINSETTIA CAKE

Scarlet poinsettias brighten your home with living color at Christmas time, and here they're used to brighten a cake. The vivid "petals", holly leaves and berries are all easy to make from marzipan.

For this cake you'll need marzipan, as made on page 52, large and medium-size daisy cookie cutters, Hexagon Pan with center hole, decorating tubes 8 and 10, decorating bags. Two cups buttercream icing, food coloring, a sharp knife and an artists' brush. You also need confectioners' sugar, a rolling pin and a fat yellow candle.

1. Prepare marzipan. One-half recipe will make the trim for this cake. Shape marzipan into a roll, and divide into thirds. Tint two-thirds red, reserving a small amount to tint yellow for centers, and tint the remaining third green.

2. Dust working surface with powdered sugar and roll out red marzipan just like pie dough to ⅛" thickness. Cut out six large and six medium flowers. With hands, shape thirty red balls for holly berries, and six yellow balls for flower centers.

3. Make leaves. Roll out green marzipan about ⅛" thick. Trace holly leaf pattern on thin cardboard, cut it out and lay on marzipan. Cut out eighteen leaves with sharp knife. Let all dry overnight.

4. Bake cake. Cool and ice with buttercream. Place on cake plate and pipe tube 10 ball border around the base, tube 8 ball border around center hole.

5. Glaze and assemble trim. Combine ½ cup corn syrup with one or two tablespoons of water and bring to a boil. Brush lightly over marzipan pieces. While glaze is still sticky, stack medium on large flowers, top with yellow balls. Then arrange flowers, leaves and berries on cake. Place candle in center hole. Serves twelve.

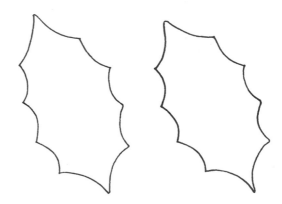

Holly leaf pattern

55

PICK A PEAR TREE CENTERPIECE

All through the twelve days of Christmas, enjoy this pretty pear tree as a centerpiece, a conversation starter, a party decoration.

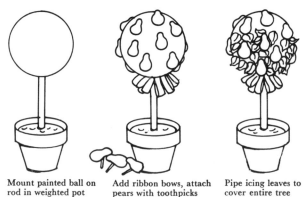

Mount painted ball on rod in weighted pot

Add ribbon bows, attach pears with toothpicks

Pipe icing leaves to cover entire tree

You'll need a clean clay 4″ flowerpot, 6″ styrofoam ball, styrofoam circle 2″ deep cut to fit base of pot, ¼″ dowel rod 12″ long, 3½ cups royal icing, tube 70, decorating bags, whole cloves, food coloring, toothpicks, ribbon and glue. Use stones to weight pot.

1. Prepare one recipe marzipan and shape pears as described on page 52. Insert clove in base and toothpick in side of each pear. Let dry overnight.

2. Cover ball with thinned royal icing. Dry overnight. Fit styrofoam circle into base of pot. Wrap dowel rod with ribbon, leaving 3″ uncovered at each end.

3. Insert rod into center of ball and push in 3″. Attach ribbon loops to base of ball with glue. Put glue on other end of rod and insert into center of styrofoam in pot. Fill pot with alternate layers of stones and icing, ending with icing. Dry overnight.

4. Tint and glaze pears as on page 52. Let dry one hour. Place pears on ball, trimming toothpicks if necessary. Cover ball with tube 70 leaves, starting at base and working up. Glue ribbon trim on pot.

WREATHED IN MARZIPAN

This festive cake crowns your holiday table with a bountiful array of luscious-looking marzipan fruits.

For this Christmas Wreath Cake, make two recipes of marzipan into fruit as directed on page 52. This makes seventy-five pieces. Prepare fruit at least forty-eight hours ahead. You also need ½ cup buttercream icing, food coloring, tube 70, aluminum foil, a 10″ taper, and a 3½″ x 8½″ Turk's Head Mold.

YULE POUND CAKE

2 cups sifted cake flour
1½ teaspoons baking powder
½ teaspoon salt
1 cup butter
1½ teaspoons vanilla extract
1½ cups sugar
4 eggs, well beaten
½ cup milk
8 ounce jar apricot preserves for glaze

1. Sift flour, baking powder, and salt together, and set aside. Cream butter with vanilla extract. Gradually add sugar, creaming until fluffy. Add eggs in thirds, beating thoroughly after each addition.

2. Beating only until smooth after each addition, alternately add dry ingredients in thirds and milk in halves. Turn batter into greased Turk's Head Mold.

3. Bake at 325° forty minutes or until cake tests done. Cool ten minutes in pan on wire rack, then remove and cool completely.

4. Put cake on serving plate and spoon on hot glaze (heat preserves to a boil and strain). Arrange glazed marzipan fruit around cake and pipe tube 70 leaves. Set candle in cake center in crumpled foil. Serve with sweetened whipped cream to twelve.

MARZIPAN ANGELS HERALD THE HOLIDAYS

Early in the holiday season, set the festive mood with this whimsical party cake trimmed with flowers, glowing with candles and topped with lovable little angels. Flowers, leaves and angels are all fashioned of versatile, easy to model marzipan. The result is an appealing dessert for your December bridge luncheon or special holiday tea.

To make it, you'll need one-third of the basic recipe for marzipan (see page 52 for recipe and technique), holly leaf pattern on page 55, a 5-petaled flower cutter, decorating tubes 6 and 12, decorating bags, four cups buttercream icing, and food coloring. You also need 8″ square cake pans, toothpicks, orange stick, a sharp knife, a small brush, and egg white to use as "glue" in joining marzipan angel pieces.

MAKING ANGELS

Make the angel figures first, since some parts need to dry for an hour before assembling. To make two angels and the flower and leaf trim for cake, prepare one-third of the basic marzipan recipe on page 52.

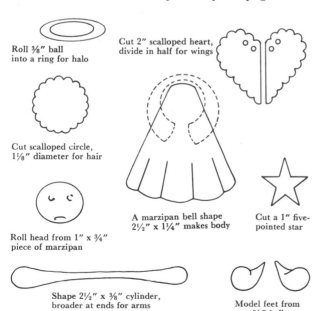

Roll ⅜″ ball into a ring for halo

Cut 2″ scalloped heart, divide in half for wings

Cut scalloped circle, 1⅛″ diameter for hair

Roll head from 1″ x ¾″ piece of marzipan

A marzipan bell shape 2½″ x 1¼″ makes body

Cut a 1″ five-pointed star

Shape 2½″ x ⅜″ cylinder, broader at ends for arms

Model feet from two ⅜″ balls

1. Shape marzipan into a roll about 1″ in diameter. Pinch off about 2″ and roll about ¹⁄₁₆″ thick; cut out two hearts. Cut each into two pieces, to make two pairs of wings. Cut toothpicks in two and insert halves in the wings at marked spots, to secure wings to body. Let dry an hour.

2. Pinch off similar piece and tint yellow, with knead-in technique described on page 52. Roll out to $\frac{1}{16}$″ thickness, cut out stars, and two scalloped circles for hair. Cut out twelve dots for flower centers, using tip of tube 12. Keep hair circles under damp towel. Let other pieces dry one hour.

3. Pinch off a 1″ x ¾″ piece for head, add just a dot of copper color on a toothpick and knead in to get flesh color. Roll into ball and poke two holes for eyes with a toothpick. Immediately brush top of head with egg white and press on hair circle.

4. Divide remaining untinted marzipan in half, adding leftover yellow pieces to one half and kneading in green color. Tint remaining half by kneading in red color. From each color, roll a 2½″ x ⅜″ cylinder, broader at the ends, and curve it to make arms. Let arms dry one hour.

5. Pinch off a small portion from each color and roll into two ⅜″ balls. Shape these into feet, flattening one end and rounding the other to look like tip of a shoe. Let dry an hour.

6. Take a piece of red marzipan about 2″ long, roll out to $\frac{1}{16}$″ thickness, cut out twelve flowers. Brush yellow centers with egg white and attach to flowers, let dry an hour. Add leftover bits to red portion.

7. Take similar piece of green marzipan, roll out $\frac{1}{16}$″ thick, cut out holly pieces using pattern, page 55. Let dry an hour. Return leftover pieces to main portion of green marzipan.

8. Shape two angel bodies, one red and one green, using about 2½″ x 1¼″ piece for each one. Press folds in skirt with orange stick or brush handle. Insert toothpick in top of body, brush with egg white.

9. Assemble angels. Brush arms with egg white, press on shoulders of body portion. Press head on toothpick inserted in body. Brush halo with egg white and put on top of hair. Put feet on bottom of body, gluing with a touch of egg white. Brush star with egg white and place at ends of arms.

DECORATING THE CAKE

Bake two layers in 8″ square cake pan, fill and ice with buttercream. Arrange leaves and flowers on sides of cake before icing sets. Pipe tube 6 ball border around bottom of cake. Insert candles in cake and position angels in front of them. Serves twelve.

GIVE A BASKET OF STRAWBERRIES

Imagine their pleasant surprise when your favorite friends or relatives receive this prize basket of strawberries. A glazed mint sugar basket with its realistic strawberries is a marvelous way to give marzipan candy for gifts at Christmas or any time of the year. If stored carefully, the basket will last for years of future enjoyment, because of the acrylic spray coating used to seal it. Best of all, it is easy to make.

For the basket you need ⅙ recipe of mint sugar (a 3″ diameter ball), rolling pin, food colors, a sharp knife, an artists' brush, 2″ x 3″ x 3″ styrofoam block, egg white, waxed paper and acrylic spray coating. To make strawberries you need ⅓ batch of marzipan, a clean sponge, red granulated sugar, food color and artificial Marzipan Leaves.

MINT SUGAR RECIPE

3 envelopes unflavored gelatin (3 tablespoons)
1 cup warm water
½ cup cornstarch
3 pounds confectioners' sugar
2 to 3 drops oil of peppermint

Dissolve gelatin in warm water and strain into a bowl through a fine sieve. Add peppermint oil, then blend in cornstarch and a little powdered sugar. Add sugar a little at a time, until the mixture becomes very smooth. When mint sugar is of the correct consistency, store in tightly closed plastic bag.

To tint, add small amounts of food color with toothpick and knead into mixture with hands.

To roll out mint sugar, always dust your hands, work surface and rolling pin with cornstarch first; then roll to desired thickness. Cut out pattern pieces immediately, since mint sugar is very quick drying.

Store unused mint sugar in a tightly closed plastic bag. It will keep ten days or more.

BASKET

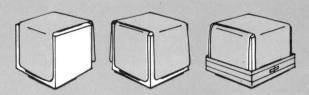

1. Tint a 3″ diameter ball of mint sugar. We used a touch of gold and brown to achieve the beige color.

2. Roll out 1/16″ thick. Roll out and cut only one piece at a time, leaving the rest in tightly closed plastic bag. Work very quickly to avoid drying. Cut two pieces 6½″ x 2½″ and four strips 3″ x ½″. Score large pieces on fold lines, 1⅝″ in from 2½″ edges, being careful not to cut all the way through.

3. Assemble on styrofoam block brushing on egg white to glue pieces (see diagram above). Wrap a wax paper band around the basket to hold its shape while drying. After it is completely dry (about twenty-four hours), spray with glaze.

STRAWBERRIES

1. Form red-tinted marzipan (see page 52 for recipe and tinting instructions) into a ½″ cylinder, cut into 1″ lengths. Roll each piece into a ball and pinch end to give it berry shape.

2. Roll lightly on damp sponge, then in red granulated sugar. Push a strawberry leaf in top. Let dry about twenty-four hours. Arrange in basket and trim with a few blossoms made with royal icing and tube 102 and a fluffy bow. Makes thirty berries.

Holiday Trims
for your home

2. Cut shapes. Roll out about ⅛″ thick, one color at a time. Cut a 6″ circle with a 4″ center hole. Cut three sizes of daisies with Daisy Cookie cutters, about one dozen of each size. To cut centers, use tube 2A for large daisy, tube 1A for medium and tube 12 for small. Let some flowers dry flat, others in and on curved surface. Let all pieces dry thoroughly.

3. Assemble. Glue centers in flowers. Set candle within ring and attach flowers with glue. Remove candle and spray with acrylic coating.

MATCHING PLACE CARD HOLDERS

Each is made with two medium and one large daisy and two ball centers. Cut medium daisies in half. Dry all flat. Glue half-daisies at right angles and prop until dry. (See diagram.) Glue in centers. Using large daisy as base, glue right angle daisies to it, placing a card between them. Spray, then remove card. Stored carefully, they can be enjoyed for many years.

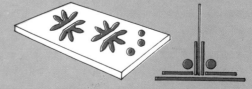

To BRIGHTEN YOUR HOME or to give to a friend, the trims shown here and on the following pages can be made right in your kitchen. They're so pretty you'll use them for parties all year long.

CANDLE CENTERPIECE

Make a mint sugar candle ring and matching place card holders to brighten the holidays!

You will need one recipe of mint sugar (page 60), Daisy Cookie cutters in three sizes, food colors, airplane glue and acrylic spray (buy in hardware stores). Have at hand plastic bags, a sharp knife, and a 3″ diameter candle. Also tubes 1A, 2A, 12.

1. Divide batch into thirds. Knead in colors. Keep each color tightly wrapped in plastic bag until ready to use. Mint sugar dries quickly!

MAKE A GAY HOLIDAY WREATH!

Display a festive wreath on a door or wall to add to the Christmas spirit! Made of mint sugar and glazed to preserve its beauty, it will reflect your creativity for many years.

These two wreaths are very similar in construction to the candle ring on page 61. Daisy wreath takes one recipe of mint sugar and Holly wreath takes one-half recipe. You'll also need a sharp knife, Daisy cookie cutters, holly and bird patterns, airplane glue, ribbon, food colors, decorating tubes 1A, 2A, 10 and 12, wire for hanging and acrylic spray coating.

Continued on page 65

Continued on page 65

TURN A PLAIN CANDLE INTO A WORK OF ART

GLOWING CANDLES, a beautiful and traditional part of Christmas, are easy to dress up with unique trims made of mint sugar. The procedure for making these jolly trims is similar for all. One recipe of mint sugar will make trims for five candles.

General instructions: You will need one recipe of mint sugar (page 60), food colors, clear acrylic spray coating, airplane glue, plastic wrap, patterns on page 65, star patterns on page 18, gum paste blossom cutters, sharp knife, and tubes 2A, 5, 9, and 12. Divide batch into five portions and color each. We used yellow, red, green, blue and peach. Roll out a small piece at a time ⅛" thick, keeping other portions in tightly closed plastic. Cut pieces out using patterns or cutters, working very quickly to avoid drying. After mint sugar pieces are cut and dried, spray and glue to candles. Use 2¾" round and square candles.

The square candle bases are made with 4" square and 3½" square pieces of mint sugar. The round bases use 4½" diameter and 3¾" diameter circles. Scallops on the smaller base pieces are cut with large end of a tube. Dry flat, glue together and glaze.

MAKE MILK CARTON CANDLES

If you enjoy candlemaking, you might want to make your own 4" high square candles from milk cartons. Don't attempt a taller candle in the carton because the weight of the wax bends the carton out of shape. About one pound of wax makes a 4" candle.

1. As the wax is melting in a double boiler, cut a clean

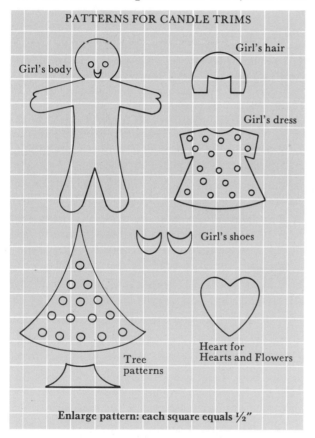

PATTERNS FOR CANDLE TRIMS

Girl's body · Girl's hair · Girl's dress · Girl's shoes · Tree patterns · Heart for Hearts and Flowers

Enlarge pattern: each square equals ½"

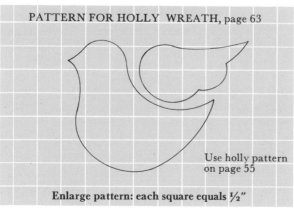

PATTERN FOR HOLLY WREATH, page 63

Use holly pattern on page 55

Enlarge pattern: each square equals ½"

quart milk carton down to 5" tall. Punch a very small hole in the bottom of the carton and push a wick through. (Buy a wick at hobby shop.) Tie a loose knot in the wick on outside of the carton. Lay a pencil across the top of the carton and tie wick to it, pulling it straight. Spread newspaper over work area.

2. After the wax has melted, turn off heat. Add color. Let wax cool ten to fifteen minutes, then pour slowly into carton. (If wax is too hot it will melt carton.) Let candle cool thoroughly. If a depression forms near the wick, remelt the leftover wax and fill only to top of previously poured wax. When fully cooled, tear carton away, polish candle with nylon stocking.

TRIM THE CANDLES

Hearts and Flowers. Blossom cutter is used for blue flowers. Leaves are shaped with same cutter and cut into five pieces. The mini blossom cutter is used for heart center. Cut flower centers with tube 12. Dry flat and assemble. Glue pieces to candle.

Little Girl. The eyes are cut with tube 5, dots with tube 9. The mouth is a sliver of mint sugar. Dry flat, assemble, glue to candle.

Holly Berry. Berries are cut with tube 2A and dried flat. Dry leaves on plastic-wrapped candle to curve.

Star Struck. Use star patterns in two sizes given on page 18. Dry on candle to curve. Glue to candle.

Tree Parade. Holes in tree are cut with tube 9. Cut star from smaller star pattern on page 18. Dry all on candle to curve. Glue to candle.

HOLIDAY WREATHS *(continued)*
DAISY WREATH

1. Divide one batch of mint sugar into thirds. Leave one-third white, tint two-thirds blue and green.

2. Cut an 8" diameter white circle with 5½" center cut out. Cut hole in top of ring with tube 10. Cut out daisies, about twelve of each size. Knead yellow in leftover white mint sugar for centers, cut with tubes 2A, 1A and 12. Dry all flat. Attach centers with glue.

3. Pass ribbon through hole in ring and glue. Glue on all daisies. Dry thoroughly, then spray.

HOLLY WREATH

1. Using one-half batch of mint sugar, color a small portion red for bird and berries. Color the rest two-thirds dark green and one-third light green for leaves.

2. Cut wreath ring the same as for the daisy wreath. Cut about sixty holly leaves. Let some dry flat, others on a curved surface. Cut pieces for bird. Cut berries with tube 2A. Let all pieces dry thoroughly.

3. Assemble. Loop wire through hole in ring for hanging. Glue wing to bird body, add tube 10 eye. Glue a few flat leaves to ring, then secure assembled bird. Add more leaves. Spray, glue on bow.

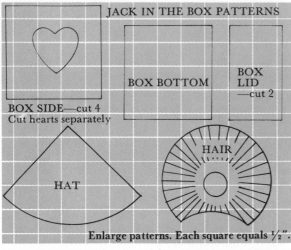

JACK IN THE BOX PATTERNS

BOX SIDE—cut 4
Cut hearts separately

BOX BOTTOM

BOX LID —cut 2

HAT

HAIR

Enlarge patterns. Each square equals ½".

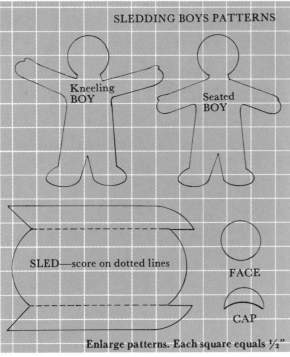

SLEDDING BOYS PATTERNS

Kneeling BOY

Seated BOY

SLED—score on dotted lines

FACE

CAP

Enlarge patterns. Each square equals ½"

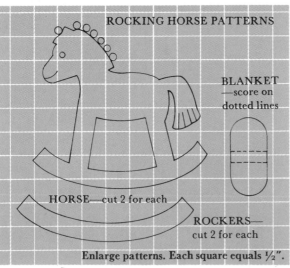

ROCKING HORSE PATTERNS

BLANKET —score on dotted lines

HORSE—cut 2 for each

ROCKERS— cut 2 for each

Enlarge patterns. Each square equals ½".

ENCHANTING MINT SUGAR TOYS

Dress up a table or mantel with a group of these delightful little toys! They'll enchant young and old.

To make all toys shown you need one recipe mint sugar (page 60), food colors, patterns, heavy and fine cloth-covered florist's wire, four tablespoons royal icing, 1½" styrofoam ball, gum paste blossom cutters, plastic bags, tubes 6, 10 and 12, styrofoam blocks, acrylic spray coating and airplane glue.

Set aside a 2" ball of mint sugar and divide remainder into four portions. Knead a different color into each. We used red, yellow, blue and green. Leave one half of 2" ball white and color other half peach. Keep tightly closed in plastic bag.

When cutting, roll out only a small piece at a time, ½₆" thick. Work very quickly, mint sugar dries fast.

JACK IN THE BOX

1. To make "Jack", wind a 12" piece of heavy florist's wire around your finger to make spring. Insert one end into 1½" styrofoam ball, the other in styrofoam block. Paint head and spring with thinned royal icing. Cut facial features with tube 6, mouth is a sliver. Cut hat, roll into cone and glue. Cut hair, then cut "fringe" ⅓ of the way in all around. Dry on 1½" ball to shape. When pieces dry, assemble with glue.

2. Cut box pieces and dry. Glue hearts to sides. Assemble; prop until dry. Glue lid open at 90° angle.

3. Cut flowers with blossom cutters, centers with tube 12. Glue 4" piece of thin florist's wire to each flower. Use mini-blossom cutter for flower on hat.

4. Assemble. Glue a ½" thick piece of styrofoam into bottom of box. Insert spring and flower wires into styrofoam. Spray with acrylic coating.

SLEDDING BOYS

1. Cut sled from pattern. Score along fold lines, being careful not to cut through. Dry on styrofoam block.

2. Cut boys. Bend carefully and dry on block. Dry face and hat flat, then glue to body. Decorate boys' snowsuits with small pieces of white mint sugar.

3. Glue boys to sled. Spray with acrylic coating.

ROCKING HORSE

1. Cut horses and rockers. Fringe tail. To dry horses, cut square piece of styrofoam diagonally, then cut that angle in half. This gives you one block for each side of horse. Lay blocks on table with points facing each other. Place horse flat on table with legs and rockers extending up onto block. Be sure heads of two horse sides are facing same direction.

2. Cut mane with tube 10 and eyes with tube 6. When all pieces are dry, glue horse sides together. Attach mane, eyes and rockers.

3. Cut blanket. Score to fit horse's back. Attach with glue. When dry, spray with acrylic coating.

GAY CANDLE HOLDERS
BRIGHTEN
YOUR HOLIDAY TABLE

These colorful mint sugar candle holders dress up any table whether for a children's party or holiday buffet. Make a pair or more for a distinctive addition to your centerpiece.

Use regular dinner candles for the Elf holders, slim tapers for the others. A 1″ wide strip of mint sugar is wrapped around each candle or taper (except for the Angel holder) and dried to form a ring to receive the candle. For the Elf and Daisy holders, this ring is glued to a circular base to insure stability. Star candle does not need a base.

For all holders shown, you need one recipe of mint sugar, food colors, patterns, Daisy and tiny blossom cookie cutters, tubes 2A and 7, sharp knife, wax paper, styrofoam blocks, plastic bags, dinner candles and tapers, airplane glue and acrylic spray glaze.

Continued on page 70

Divide mint sugar into six portions. Color five of the portions different colors, leaving one white. Divide white portion and color a small piece of it peach. Roll out only a small piece of mint sugar at a time $\frac{1}{16}''$ thick. Mint sugar dries quickly so keep unused portions wrapped tightly in plastic.

Elf candle holder. Cut pieces from patterns. Insert candle into styrofoam block. Drape elf body around candle to dry. Apply face, hat and cuffs with glue. Eyes are cut with tube 7 and pompom with tube 2A.

To make base, cut a $3\frac{3}{4}''$ diameter circle. Cut scallops with tube and round off points. Cut a $2\frac{3}{8}''$ diameter circle and a $1''$ wide strip to fit around bottom of candle. Wrap strip around candle to dry and use wax paper strip to hold in place. When dry, glue base together and elf to base. Spray.

Daisy candle holder. Cut three medium daisies for each holder with cutter. Cut centers with tube 2A. Glue together and dry on curved surface. For base, cut one large daisy, a $3''$ diameter circle and **a** $1''$ wide strip to fit around bottom of taper. Dry strip

around taper, using wax paper strip to hold in place. Glue all pieces together and spray.

Star candle holder. Cut half-star shapes from pattern, three left and three right for each holder. Cut a $1''$ wide strip to fit around taper. Dry strip on taper using wax paper strip to hold in place. Glue together, spacing star pieces evenly around taper. Spray.

Angel candle holder. For base, cut two $3\frac{1}{4}''$ diameter circles and cut scallops on one with base of tube.

Form a $1''$ ball of mint sugar and press base of taper into it. Using light-weight cardboard, cut pattern for body (minus head) and tape together into a cone around taper. Cover with wax paper and slip over taper. Cut mint sugar body and form around cone. Cut arms and attach with glue. Cut face, hair, collar and wings and glue to body. Apply features and trim on dress using small pieces of mint sugar. Add flower, cut with blossom cutter. Dry, then remove from cardboard cone. Glue ball holding taper to the base, then slip angel over paper and glue to base. Spray with acrylic coating.

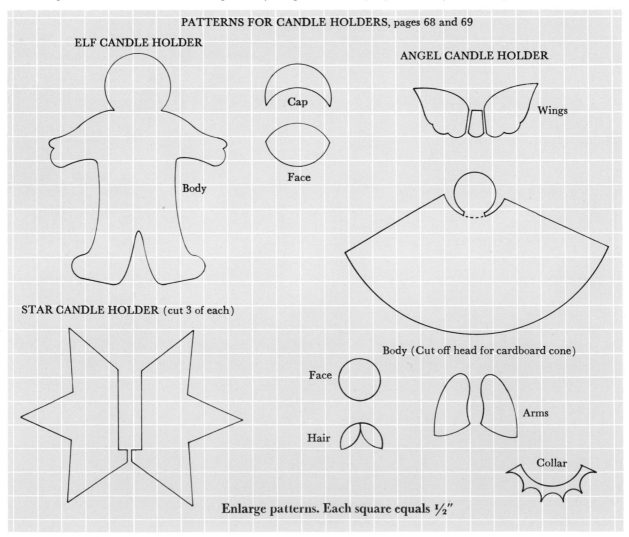

PATTERNS FOR CANDLE HOLDERS, pages 68 and 69

ELF CANDLE HOLDER

ANGEL CANDLE HOLDER

Cap

Face

Body

Wings

Body (Cut off head for cardboard cone)

STAR CANDLE HOLDER (cut 3 of each)

Face

Hair

Arms

Collar

Enlarge patterns. Each square equals $\frac{1}{2}''$

Holiday Works of Art

Make this Candle-lit Madonna picture, or the one of Children at Work on page 73 and you will have a lovely dimensional scene to display in your home. Made of Color Flow icing, if handled and stored carefully they can be enjoyed for years.

You need one recipe of Color Flow icing (page 16) for each plaque, food colors, patterns, tubes 1, 2, 15 and 655, wax paper or plastic wrap, stiff mat board, sugar cubes, and tacks or tiny nails. You also need frames for your art. We used an oval frame 11″ x 9″ and a rectangular frame 9½″ x 7½″.

Cut mat board to fit frames. Secure with tacks or tiny nails and add a hanging wire. Follow the general Color Flow directions on page 16.

Continued on next page

COLOR FLOW PICTURES *continued*
CANDLE-LIT MADONNA

1. Tape patterns on cardboard, covering with wax paper or plastic wrap and taping securely. Outline star in yellow with tube 1, Child in brown with tube 1. Outline all other areas in brown with Tube 2. Let dry one or two hours, then flow in colors with softened Color Flow icing.

2. Let dry forty-eight hours, then turn over very carefully and peel off wax paper. Outline backs ¼″ in from edge and flow in white Color Flow icing.

3. When dry, (at least forty-eight hours) turn over carefully and add all details with tube 1.

4. To attach, trace outline of tree pattern on transparent paper, cut out and place in position in frame. Use pin to mark position lightly, then pipe dabs of Color Flow icing inside marks on all sides and center. Lay tree section in position, then pipe dabs of icing on tree to attach Madonna. Attach star with a ball of icing. Let dry thoroughly and hang for all to admire.

CHILDREN AT WORK

1. Follow directions in steps 1 and 2 above, outlining all pieces with gold icing and tube 1.

2. Pipe details on clothes, bows and popcorn with tube 1. Make leaves in flower pot with tube 655 and wreath with tube 15.

3. To assemble, trace outlines of patterns on transparent paper. Cut out and place in position in frame. Mark lightly with pin. Pieces are set in five levels for dimensional effect, held with mounds of icing in varied heights. Gently place rug and window in position first with dabs of icing. Then add pieces in levels two, three, four and five (see patterns). Fifth level rests on sugar cubes and icing. When thoroughly dry, hang on wall.

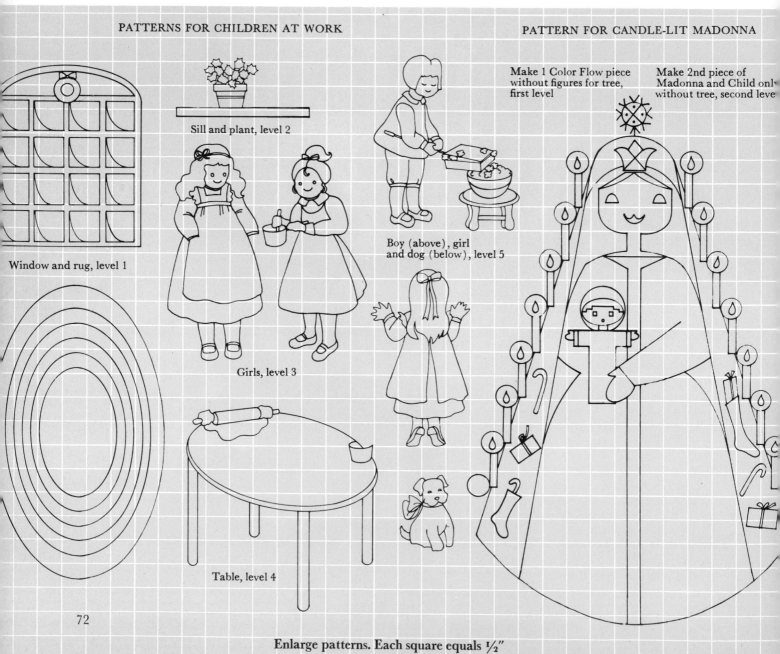

PATTERNS FOR CHILDREN AT WORK

PATTERN FOR CANDLE-LIT MADONNA

Window and rug, level 1

Sill and plant, level 2

Girls, level 3

Table, level 4

Boy (above), girl and dog (below), level 5

Make 1 Color Flow piece without figures for tree, first level

Make 2nd piece of Madonna and Child only without tree, second level

Enlarge patterns. Each square equals ½″

Children at Work

CHRISTMAS IS A TIME for making people happy. Even a child as young as six will have a wonderful time preparing holiday treats all by himself (with just a little help from you)—and feel a special pride in serving them to family and friends.

Start by rolling up your sleeves, scrubbing your hands, and putting on an apron. Now set out on the counter everything you need to make this pretty Christmas cake and cupcakes.

Here are the foods you'll need:

A box of cake mix
One or two eggs
(as the box directs)
Two cans of ready-to-use frosting

One 4-ounce package of shredded coconut
Six red candied cherries
Green and red liquid food color
Butter, for greasing pans

You will need these tools, plus thirteen candles.

A large mixing bowl for mixing the cake
Three smaller bowls
A large spoon for batter
Smaller spoons for mixing frosting
Two 6″ round cake pans
A cupcake pan
Fluted paper liners for cupcake pan

Wax paper
An electric mixer
Measuring cup
A small spatula
Racks for cooling cakes
A small plastic bag
A plastic decorating bag fitted with tube 13
Kitchen scissors

START BY BAKING THE CAKES

Mix the cake batter just as the box directs. Mother can help you do this and will turn on the oven. Use your fingers to butter the inside of both round pans.

1. Pour about half the batter into the two round pans. Put the fluted paper liners into the cupcake pan, and pour the rest of the batter into the cupcake pan. This should make ten or twelve cupcakes. Bake the cakes as the box directs. Mother will take them out of the oven and cool them on the racks.

2. Cut each cherry in half with the scissors. Cut each half into three "petals". Set aside.

3. Tint the coconut green. Put the coconut into the plastic bag. Now add about sixteen drops of green food coloring. Twist the top of the bag closed and squeeze it repeatedly to spread the coloring through the coconut. Tear off a sheet of wax paper about two feet long, and spread the coconut on it to dry.

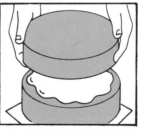

4. Place one 6″ layer, top side down, on a piece of wax paper. Open one can of frosting and spread about one-third of it on the cake, almost to the edge. Set the second layer on top, right side up.

5. Now frost the side of the layer cake, using about one-third of the remaining frosting. Use the spatula to coat evenly. Do not frost the top yet.

6. Make a "path" of the green coconut about 3″ wide on the wax paper. Slide the spatula under the cake to loosen it from its wax paper and put one hand on the bottom of cake, the other on top. Roll the cake like a wheel on the coconut "path". Like magic the sides are covered with coconut!

7. Put the cake on a plate and frost the top, using the rest of the frosting in the can. Make flowers all around the edge of the cake with the cherry "petals" using five petals for each. Push a candle into the center. Your cake will slice into six delicious pieces.

NOW DECORATE THE CUPCAKES

Cupcakes are fun to decorate, and you'll enjoy using a real, professional decorating bag.

1. **Open the second can** of frosting and as evenly as possible, divide it into thirds, putting one-third into each small bowl. Set one bowl in the refrigerator to use for the borders. Now tint one bowl of frosting green. Put about four drops of green food coloring into the bowl, and stir thoroughly for an even tint.

2. **Frost half** of the cupcakes green. Hold the cupcake in one hand and swirl the green frosting over the top with the spatula. Now tint the second bowl of frosting pink, using four drops of red food coloring, and stirring it just as you did for the green. Frost the remaining cupcakes.

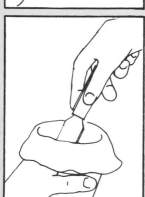

3. **Now get ready** to decorate! Fit the decorating bag with tube 13. (Let Mother help.) Take the bowl of white frosting out of the refrigerator. Hold the bag in your left hand and turn the top of the bag down like a cuff. With the spatula, dip mounds of icing out of the bowl and into the bag, pressing the spatula against your thumb to push it into the bag. When it is all in the bag, turn the top up and twist to close.

4. **Hold a cupcake** in your left hand and the bag in your right. Look at the picture to see the correct position. Touch the tube to the edge of the cupcake, squeeze the bag gently and move it up and down in a zigzag motion to make the border. As you squeeze the bag, turn the cupcake with your left hand.

Push a candle in the center of each cupcake, and put them on a plate. Serve your beautiful Christmas Cake and cupcakes at an afternoon party, or for a special dessert. Weren't they fun to decorate?

I MADE IT MYSELF!

CHRISTMAS HOLLY CLUSTERS*

Here's a way to make red and green candy that's good to eat and good for you! It's nice to have a friend help form the clusters after they are cooked.

Before you start, scrub your hands and get out everything you'll need. First, set out all the ingredients listed in the recipe.

You'll also need:

Wax paper
A big saucepan
Tablespoons for forming clusters

A large spoon for stirring
Measuring spoons
A measuring cup

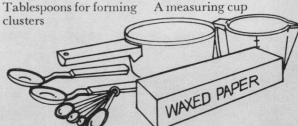

HOLLY CLUSTER RECIPE

1 stick (½ cup) butter or margarine
30 large marshmallows
¼ teaspoon green food coloring
4½ cups cornflakes
⅓ cup red cinnamon candies

1. **Spread pieces of wax paper,** about one foot long on a table, one for you, one for your helper. Measure the cinnamon candies and set them on the table.

2. **Measure the corn flakes** and put them in a pile on another piece of wax paper.

3. **Unwrap the butter** (or margarine) and put it in the saucepan. Ask Mother to turn on the burner to low. Put the saucepan on the burner and watch carefully until the butter starts to melt.

4. **Add the marshmallows** to the saucepan. Stir until the butter and marshmallows are completely melted.

5. **Turn off the heat,** add the food coloring, and stir until the mixture is evenly colored. Pour in the cornflakes and stir just until they are coated.

6. **Pick up portions** of candy with a tablespoon and drop them on the wax paper you prepared in Step 1. Your friend will help you with this, and with Step 7.

7. **Press several red cinnamon candies** on each cluster. Let the clusters dry about one hour. There should be about thirty-six clusters.

*A thank you to **Mrs. Dean McGrew** of Randolph, Nebraska, for this recipe.

I MADE IT MYSELF!

POPCORN BALLS!

Everyone loves popcorn balls! Give them to friends, hang them on the tree, put a big tray of them near the door for company. Ask your friends or family to help and get set for fun.

Set out all the ingredients in the recipe and wash your hands. You can buy the popped corn or have a popping party the night before. Now get these things ready:

WAXED PAPER
PLASTIC WRAP

Two large mixing bowls	Wax paper
A large saucepan with cover	Butter for buttering your hands
Measuring cups	Clear plastic wrap
Measuring spoons	Red and green ribbon
Two large spoons for stirring	
A candy thermometer	
Scissors	

POPCORN BALL RECIPE

Ask Mother to turn on the oven and burner.

    4 quarts popped corn
    1 cup sugar
    1 cup light corn syrup
    ½ cup water
    2 tablespoons butter or margarine

1. **Divide the popped corn** into the two large bowls. Set them in a very low oven to warm.

2. **Put all the rest** of the ingredients into the saucepan. Set the saucepan on very low heat and stir until all the sugar is dissolved.

3. **Put the cover on the saucepan,** raise the heat, and bring the mixture to boiling. (You can hear it boil.) Remove the cover and place the candy thermometer in the pan. Continue cooking, without stirring, until the thermometer says 245°. Take the pan off the heat.

4. **Ask Mother to remove** the large bowls of popped corn from the oven. Now pour the cooked syrup slowly over the popped corn, dividing it as evenly as possible between the two bowls. Stir the corn until it is evenly coated with syrup. (A friend can also stir.)

5. **As soon as the corn** is cool enough to touch, butter your hands and shape the corn into balls. Press firmly to make nice, round shapes.

6. **Set the balls** on sheets of wax paper to dry. Tear off about one foot of plastic wrap, set a popcorn ball in the middle, and wrap the ball, twisting the wrap at the top to close. Continue until all the balls are wrapped. Tie a ribbon on each wrapped ball. You'll have about two dozen.

DOUBLE CHOCOLATE DROPS

If you like chocolate, you'll love these cookies! You'll have a lot of fun making them, right from scratch, and just as much fun serving them to friends. First get everything ready. You'll need these tools.

A large mixing bowl Cookie sheets

A large spoon for stirring A teaspoon

A measuring cup A smaller bowl and spoon

Measuring spoons   for frosting

Wax paper   A small spatula

Paper toweling   Scissors

A flour sifter

You'll also need all the ingredients listed in the recipe. Scrub your hands, put on an apron and begin!

CHOCOLATE DROP RECIPE

1 stick soft butter   1 cup sugar
½ teaspoon salt   1 egg
1 teaspoon vanilla   ¾ cup buttermilk
1¾ cup flour, sifted ½ teaspoon soda
½ cup cocoa

1. Put the butter (or margarine) in the large bowl. Add the sugar, crack the egg on the side of the bowl and drop that in. Stir until completely mixed.

2. Measure the buttermilk into the measuring cup. Add the soda, salt and vanilla to the cup. Now pour this mixture into the bowl and mix well again.

3. Put some flour into the sifter, and sift quite a large pile onto a square of wax paper. Now spoon the sifted flour into a measuring cup. When you have measured one cup, dump it onto a second square of wax paper. Measure ¾ cup of the sifted flour and add it to the second square of wax paper. Add the cocoa to the second square of wax paper. Now put about half the cocoa and sifted flour mixture back in the sifter and sift it into the bowl. Stir the contents of bowl thoroughly. Put the rest of the cocoa-flour mixture in the sifter and sift into the bowl. Stir thoroughly again.

4. Place the bowl of dough in the refrigerator for an hour. Ask Mother to preheat the oven to 400°.

5. Butter the cookie sheets. Remove the dough from the refrigerator. Drop the dough by teaspoonfuls on the cookie sheets, leaving about 2″ between mounds. Bake about ten minutes. They are done when a light touch of a finger leaves no mark. Let the cookies cool on the cookie sheets for a few minutes, then remove them with a spatula and place on paper towels. You will have about forty cookies.

CHOCOLATE FROSTING RECIPE

2 tablespoons (2 ounces) soft butter or margarine
2 tablespoons cocoa
3 tablespoons warm water
1 teaspoon vanilla
1 cup confectioners' sugar
About 24 red candied cherries and 12 green
 candied cherries

1. Cut the red cherries in half with the scissors. Cut the green cherries in half, then in half again. Set aside.

2. Put the butter (or margarine), cocoa, water and vanilla into the smaller bowl. Stir until well mixed.

3. Using a tablespoon, add two or three tablespoons of the sugar at a time to the mixture in the bowl. Stir after each addition until the frosting is smooth.

4. Spread the frosting on the cookies with the spatula. Decorate each with the cherries.

FUNNY FACE COOKIES

Bake a batch of these jolly lollipop cookies and have an ice cream party!

Set out everything you need:

A roll of ready-to-bake cookie dough (without nuts or chips.)

A bread board for cutting

A sharp serrated knife

12" x 18" cookie sheets

Eighteen popsicle sticks

Paper toweling

A spatula

A can of ready-to-use vanilla frosting

Three small bowls

Red, yellow and blue liquid food coloring

Three stirring spoons

Three decorating bags each fitted with tube 3

A kitchen towel

BAKE THE COOKIES

1. Ask Mother to turn on the oven, as the label directs. Unwrap the cookie dough and place it on the bread board. Cut eighteen slices, each about ¼" thick. Lay nine of them, well spaced, on a cookie sheet. Put the uncut dough in the refrigerator.

2. Lay a popsicle stick on each cookie on the cookie sheet, then put another slice of cookie on top of the popsicle stick. Press very lightly with your fingers.

3. Repeat Step 2 until all dough is used. Bake the cookies. Have Mother remove them from the oven and cool them for a few moments. Very carefully, using the spatula, remove the cookies from the cookie sheet and lay on paper towels.

PIPE THE FUNNY FACES

1. Open the can of frosting. Put half in one bowl and tint yellow. Put half of the rest in another bowl and tint blue. Put the remaining frosting in the third bowl and tint red. Page 75 tells you how to tint.

2. Put the three colors of frosting into the three decorating bags. (Directions are on page 75.) Dampen a kitchen towel, fold it in half and lay it on the table. Place the filled bags on the towel and cover the tubes with the edge. This keeps frosting moist.

3. Pipe the hair first with yellow frosting. Hold the bag straight up and squeeze. Now add two blue dots for eyes, giving just a quick squeeze, then stopping. Add a red mouth. Keep the decorating bags you are not using under the towel.

4. Repeat Step 3 for each cookie. Let dry about an hour. Makes about eighteen happy cookie "friends".

I MADE IT MYSELF!

Festive Little Treats

Holiday hospitality means having plenty of dainty treats on hand to offer guests with a glass of wine or a cup of coffee. Here are some four-star recipes to add to your own well-loved favorites. Serve traditional cookies with old-fashioned, home made flavor, add lavish continental pastries and learn a surprising new way to create colorful cookies without touching a decorating bag. Happy baking!

SET OUT THIS GALA DESSERT BUFFET for a festive holiday party. Guests will be charmed and impressed by its appealing variety—but everything can be prepared well ahead of time.

RICH TART PASTRY*

Make these crisp, melt-in-your-mouth pastry shells to fill with chocolate, mincemeat or lemon curd.

   3 cups sifted flour
   ¾ cup sugar
   ⅛ teaspoon salt
   ¼ cup butter, firm but not hard
   3 eggs
   ½ teaspoon vanilla or 2 teaspoons
     grated lemon rind

1. Mix flour with sugar and salt and sift into a large bowl. Make a well in the center and into that put the butter, cut into large flakes, the eggs, and vanilla or lemon rind. Make a paste of the ingredients with your fingertips, working in flour mixture until a smooth firm dough is formed. Work quickly so butter does not become oily. When sides of bowl are clean, wrap dough in wax paper and chill until firm.

2. Roll chilled dough between sheets of wax paper to less than ¼″ thickness. Fit dough over outside of small tart pans, patting into shape. Prick with fork. Freeze 1½ hours before baking.

Continued on next page

3. Bake on middle shelf of 350° oven for ten to twelve minutes, or until golden. Makes two dozen 2¾" shells. Shaped tarts may be frozen before baking. Store baked shells a day or two.

APPLE MINCE FILLING

1 small apple, washed, quartered, cored, pared and chopped (about 1 cup)
1 pint jar prepared mincemeat
1 teaspoon grated lemon peel
2 teaspoons lemon juice

1. Combine ingredients in a saucepan and heat thoroughly, stirring occasionally.

2. Cool filling before using. Fills eight tarts.

3. Garnish with Brandy Hard Sauce (page 89), piped in advance with tube 4B and frozen.

ENGLISH LEMON CURD*

2 large lemons (juice and grated rind)
5 egg yolks
½ cup sugar
¼ cup butter

1. Grate lemon peel, squeeze juice and strain.

2. Combine egg yolks and sugar in top of double boiler. Add lemon juice and grated peel, then the butter a little at a time. Stir constantly until thick. This will keep in a covered jar in the refrigerator for weeks. Makes about one cup, but double the recipe to fill eight tart shells. Pipe tube 190 drop flowers of sweetened whipped cream for garnish. Freeze. Place on tarts and top with green candied cherry.

CHOCOLATE SUPREME*

1 package (6 ounces) semi-sweet chocolate pieces
4 eggs, separated
1 teaspoon hot water
4 or 5 drops vanilla
1 tablespoon brandy

1. Melt the chocolate pieces. Cool and beat in egg yolks one at a time. Add hot water, vanilla and brandy. Fold in stiffly beaten egg whites.
2. Spoon mixture into tart shells. Chill several hours preferably overnight. Fills eight tarts. Top each with a tube 4B rosette of sweetened whipped cream piped in advance and frozen. Add candied cherry.

"HURRY-UP" PETITS FOURS

No one will ever believe how quickly you decorated these festive little cakes!

Bake your favorite cake in a 12" x 18" x 1" pan. Chill in refrigerator while you mix twelve cups of buttercream. Set aside one cup of icing for flowers and leaves. Leave half the remaining icing white and divide the rest into two bowls. Tint one bowl pink, the other brown. Get out decorating bags, a small jar of apricot preserves, tubes 1D, 3, 16, 67, 140 and 190, a 2" round cookie cutter and knife.

1. **Make drop flowers** with tubes 140 and 190 and stiffened icing. Attach wax paper to back of cookie sheet with dots of icing. Hold bag straight up, give a quick squeeze, stop pressure and lift tube. Center each flower with a tube 3 yellow dot. Freeze flowers.

2. **From chilled cake,** cut twenty-four round shapes with cutter, then thirty-six rectangular shapes, 1½" x 2", with knife. This allows for "crumbles".

3. **Heat the apricot preserves** to boiling, strain through a sieve, and while still warm, brush this glaze on the **sides only** of the cakes.

4. **Fill decorating bag,** fitted with tube 1D, with pink icing. Tape wax paper to counter and press out a 7" long strip of icing. Keep straight side of tube up. Lay the side of a round cake on beginning of the icing strip and roll cake along it until side of cake is completely covered, with a slight overlap where icing joins. Repeat with remaining round cakes.

With brown icing and tube 1D, straight side up, pipe an 8" strip on wax paper. Lay a rectangular cake on the icing and tip the cake, side following side, until all sides are covered. With practice you will be able to pipe three strips of icing, then cover sides of three cakes before piping more strips.

5. **Using white icing** and tube 16, cover tops of cakes. Start in center of round cakes and work outward in a spiral to edge. Cover rectangular cake tops with a back-and-forth motion.

6. **Press on frozen flowers,** and trim with tube 67 leaves. Sixty lovely little cakes!

PATE A CHOU* (CREAM PUFF PASTE)

1 cup water	½ teaspoon salt
½ cup butter	4 eggs
1 cup sifted flour	

1. Put the water and butter in a saucepan and bring to a boil. Lower heat, add flour and salt all at once and continue to cook, stirring constantly, until mixture leaves sides of pan and forms a ball.

2. Remove from heat and add eggs, one at a time. Be sure each is well blended before adding next.

3. To make cream puffs, butter a cookie sheet. Fit pastry bag with tube 10 or 11 and press out high mounds of paste about 1" in diameter. Allow 2" between mounds for spreading. Bake at 400° for twenty to twenty-five minutes, until they are puffed and golden and no beads of moisture show. Turn off heat. Leave puffs in closed oven for ten minutes more.

4. Remove from oven, put on rack and with a sharp knife pierce each puff to release steam. This makes about four dozen miniature cream puffs. Fill with sweetened whipped cream and ice with buttercream. Trim with drop flowers made in advance with tubes 33 and 225. Pipe tube 67 leaves.

From THE WILTON BOOK OF CLASSIC DESSERTS

HOW TO
DECORATE COOKIES
WITHOUT ICING

Make these gay little cookies, bright as Christmas morning, without a decorating tube! They're quick and easy to create using an "inlay" method and colored dough. Serve them with a flourish!

Use cutters in small and medium shapes, a sharp knife and cookie sheets. Mix a recipe of Roll-out cookie dough (page 12) and divide into four parts. Knead liquid food color into three of the portions and leave one part uncolored. Keep any dough not in use tightly wrapped in plastic.

To make holes in cookies use tube 10. Have a lightly stirred egg white, and an artist's brush ready.

Now the fun begins! Roll out about one-third of the uncolored dough and cut out shapes with the larger cutters. Cut out small shapes within the cookies, using small cutters or tube and set aside. Transfer the large shapes to ungreased cookie sheet. Immediately roll out one-third of a colored dough and cut out small shapes using the same small cutters you used for shapes within the uncolored cookies.

Set these small shapes neatly within the larger cookies on the cookie sheets.

Cut out large shapes from the remainder of the portion of colored dough and quickly set in the small uncolored shapes you had set aside. Continue working always with one-third of each color.

The gay little elf is made with a small cookie circle, top sliced off and eyes cut out. Hat band, pom pom and mouth are "appliqued" by brushing shapes with egg white before placing on cookie.

"Applique" little flower shapes on some of the cookies, "glueing" with egg white.

Bake the cookies for about eight minutes in a 375° oven. One recipe yields about five dozen.

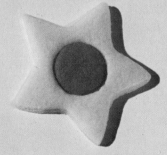

83

Here are seven mouthwatering cookies—generously shared with us by CELEBRATE! readers.

APRICOT SQUARES

Mrs. Helen Bisso of Fairview Heights, Illinois, chose this tangy fruit to spark her holiday cookies.

    1 package (8 ounces) dried apricots
    ¾ cup sugar
    ¾ cup butter or margarine
    1 cup firmly packed brown sugar
    1½ cups all-purpose flour
    1 teaspoon baking powder
    1½ cups quick oats

1. Put apricots and sugar into a saucepan. Add water to cover. Bring to boiling; boil 15 minutes.
2. Cream butter and sugar. Mix flour, baking powder. Add to creamed mixture with oats; mix well.
3. Press ⅔ of mixture into an 8″ square pan. Spread apricot mixture over first layer. Put remaining oat mixture over top.
4. Bake at 375° about 30 minutes. Cool. Cut into squares. Makes about two or three dozen cookies.

OATMEAL COCONUT CRISPS

From **Carolyn Blurton** of Brownstown, Illinois, comes a delightfully old-fashioned recipe.

    2 cups butter or margarine
    2 teaspoons vanilla extract
    2 cups sugar
    2 cups firmly packed brown sugar
    4 eggs
    3 cups sifted all-purpose flour
    2 teaspoons salt
    2 teaspoons baking soda
    6 cups quick oats
    1½ cups flaked coconut
    pecans for garnish

1. Cream butter with vanilla extract. Add sugars gradually, beating until fluffy. Add eggs, one at a time, beating well after each addition.
2. Sift flour, salt and baking soda together; stir into creamed mixture. Mix in oats and coconut.
3. Drop batter by the teaspoonful at 2″ intervals onto well-greased cookie sheets.
4. Bake at 350° about 10 minutes. Cool cookies on racks. Makes about 14 dozen cookies.

SWEDISH CHRISTMAS COOKIES

Mrs. Wilbert S. Leap, Jr., of Penns Grove, New Jersey, offers this traditional holiday cookie.

    5 cups all-purpose flour
    4 egg yolks
    4 egg yolks, hard-cooked and sieved
    2 cups butter or margarine, softened
    ½ pound (1¾ cups) confectioners' sugar
    Colored sugar

1. Put flour, egg yolks (8 uncooked, if desired), butter, and confectioners' sugar into a bowl. Mix by hand until a dough is formed. Chill dough one hour.
2. On a lightly-floured surface, use palms of hands to roll small portions of dough into strips. Each should be roughly the diameter of a pencil. Dip in colored sugar. Cut into desired lengths and shape into wreaths. Place on flour-dusted cookie sheets.
3. Bake at 350° about 10 minutes, or until golden brown. Makes fourteen to fifteen dozen cookies.

BUTTER CRISP COOKIES

Mrs. Jack Brooks of Brooksville, Kentucky, often adds holiday green or red decorations to these cookies at Christmas time.

    1 cup margarine
    1 package (3 ounces) cream cheese
    1 cup sugar
    1 egg yolk
    1 teaspoon vanilla extract
    2¾ cups all-purpose flour
    ¼ teaspoon baking powder

1. Cream margarine, cream cheese and sugar. Add egg yolk and vanilla extract; beat well. Blend flour and baking powder; mix into creamed mixture.
2. Press dough through a Spritz Cookie Press, using a variety of design discs, onto ungreased cookie sheets.
3. Bake at 350° 10 to 15 minutes, or until very pale brown around edges. Do not overbake. Cool cookies on racks. Makes about eight dozen cookies.

LACE COOKIES

These dainty cookies are a favorite of **Miss Wanda Hall** of Adrian, Georgia.

    1 cup sifted all-purpose flour
    1 cup flaked coconut or chopped nuts
    ½ cup light corn syrup
    ½ cup firmly-packed brown sugar
    ½ cup margarine
    1 teaspoon vanilla extract

1. Mix flour and coconut.
2. Combine corn syrup, brown sugar, and margarine in a heavy saucepan. Bring to a boil over medium heat, stirring constantly. Remove from heat; blend in flour mixture, a small amount at a time. Mix in vanilla.
3. Drop a scant teaspoonful of batter at intervals of about 3″ on foil-covered cookie sheets.
4. Bake at 350° 8 to 10 minutes. Cool about 4 minutes on wire rack until cookies may be easily removed from foil. Put cookies on racks covered with absorbent paper. Makes about 4½ dozen cookies.

VIENNA LINZER TARTS

Mrs. Jean Heyes of Oak Park, Illinois, sent us this intriguing recipe.

    1 cup butter or margarine
    ½ cup sugar
    4 egg yolks

4 teaspoons grated lemon peel
1 teaspoon vanilla extract
3 cups sifted all-purpose flour
½ teaspoon baking powder
Raspberry jam
Confectioners' sugar

1. Cream butter and sugar until light and fluffy. Add egg yolks, lemon peel, and vanilla extract; beat well.
2. Sift flour and baking powder together. Add to creamed mixture and mix well.
3. Chill dough four hours.
4. On a lightly-floured board, roll dough ¼″ thick. Using a star cutter, cut star shapes. Cut out centers, using a small round cutter, from half the stars. Arrange on cookie sheets.
5. Bake at 350° 10 minutes, or until lightly browned. Cool cookies on racks.
6. Spread jam on bottoms of plain stars. Dust cutout stars with confectioners' sugar and place on plain cookies. Makes about 2½ dozen Linzer Tarts.

DATE PINWHEELS

Mrs. Billy D. Harkins of Fayette, Alabama, likes to make these chewy sweets at holiday season.

Filling:
1 pound pitted dates
½ cup water
½ cup sugar

Dough:
½ cup butter or margarine
½ cup sugar
½ cup firmly-packed dark brown sugar
1 egg
½ teaspoon vanilla extract
2 cups sifted all-purpose flour
½ teaspoon baking soda
½ teaspoon salt
1 cup chopped pecans

1. For filling, combine dates, water and sugar. Cook until thick, about 10 minutes. Cool.
2. For dough, cream butter and sugars well. Add egg and vanilla extract. Beat well. Sift flour, baking soda and salt. Add in small amounts to creamed mixture, stirring until smooth each time. Add pecans.
3. Chill dough thoroughly.
4. Divide dough into four portions. Roll out each portion on a floured board, spread with a fourth of date mixture, and roll jelly-roll fashion. Wrap rolls in waxed paper. Chill three hours.
5. Cut chilled rolls into ¼″ thick slices.
6. Bake at 400° about 8 minutes. Cool cookies on racks. Makes about six to seven dozen cookies.

Top right: Oatmeal Coconut Crisps, Apricot Squares. Left: Swedish Christmas Cookies, Butter Crisp Cookies. Bottom right: Lace Cookies, Vienna Linzer Tarts, Date Pinwheels.

ELEGANT COOKIES WITH A EUROPEAN ACCENT

Serve these delicious, bite-sized morsels on any occasion you want to make memorable. Your guests will applaud their subtle flavors—and you'll gain a reputation as a master *patissiere*.

Master pastry chef Larry Olkiewicz guides you step-by-step through the recipes. He advises:

1. All flour should be sifted before adding to rest of ingredients. Use only sweet unsalted butter.

2. Use only tempered chocolate (See page 45.)

3. Rolled cookies should be rolled on a wooden board or work surface, dusted with flour. If you must roll on a plastic surface, first cover it with a clean cloth, well dusted with flour.

LINZERTOERTCHEN
Linzer Baskets

5 ounces confectioners' sugar
13 ounces sweet butter
3 egg yolks
Grated rind of 1½ lemons
18 ounces sifted flour
3½ ounces finely ground toasted almonds or hazelnuts, sifted
½ teaspoon cinnamon
Pinch of salt
4 ounces ground pistachios
4 ounces raspberry jam
Dark and milk chocolate for decorating

1. Combine and mix well by hand the first four ingredients. Combine the flour, ground nuts, salt and cinnamon and add to the first mixture. Mix well, by hand, to a firm dough. Refrigerate one hour.

2. Roll out on wooden board to ⅛″ thickness. Cut out with 1½″ diameter round cutter. Remove centers from half the shapes with base of decorating tube or tiny round cutter. Bake at 350°, eight to ten minutes or until golden. Cool.

3. Spread the whole cookies with jam and place the cut-out circles on top of them. Heat the rest of the jam, strain and brush on tops. Dip in pistachios.

4. Pipe "U"-shaped handles with dark chocolate on wax paper, using a paper cone with cut tip. Harden for ten or fifteen minutes in refrigerator. Pipe a leaf shape on opposite sides of each cookie with milk chocolate. (Cut tip of parchment cone in a downward facing "V".) Set handle on cookies, anchoring on leaves. Makes about one hundred.

NUSSKUESSCHEN
Walnut Kisses

5 egg whites
9 ounces confectioners' sugar
18 ounces soft sweet butter
1 teaspoon vanilla
Grated rind of 1½ lemons
9 ounces almond paste
24 ounces sifted flour
Pinch of salt
Almond Filling (recipe below)
Tempered dark chocolate for dipping and decorating
8 ounces toasted walnut halves

1. Combine egg whites, sugar, butter, vanilla, almond paste and rind. Beat at medium speed until volume increases by one-third. Combine flour and salt, fold

into first mixture by hand. Fill parchment paper cone fitted with tube 12. Drop dough on greased cookie sheets and bake at 360°-375° until edges are brown, center still light. Cool on rack.

2. Put Almond Filling in paper cone with cut tip. Pipe small mound of filling on half of cookies, cover with remaining cookies. Refrigerate one-half hour.

3. Dip tops of cookies in melted chocolate. Top each with a half-walnut. Pipe chocolate trim with paper cone. Recipe makes one hundred twenty-five kisses.

Almond Filling

½ cup almond paste
2 tablespoons apricot preserves
Apricot brandy

Mix all ingredients, adding apricot brandy until mixture is soft enough to use in decorating bag.

EICHENBLAETTER
Oak Leaves

½ pound almond paste
1 ounce flour
3½ ounces confectioners' sugar
1 teaspoon vanilla
4 egg whites
2 tablespoons milk
1 cup tempered dark chocolate

1. Cut a 1″ x 2″ leaf-shape hole in a 4″ square of stiff cardboard. Firmly tape a 1″ strip of cardboard to edge of stencil to use as a handle.

2. Knead first four ingredients by hand to mix well. Combine egg whites and milk and stir into first mixture. Dough should be of soft, spreadable consistency —if too stiff, add more milk. Refrigerate two hours.

3. Grease cookie sheets very thoroughly. Place stencil on sheet, spread dough in opening with spatula. Lift stencil carefully. Repeat until all dough is used. Bake at 280°, just until edges are slightly brown, about six or eight minutes. Cool completely on cookie sheets. Place cookie sheets in oven for just a minute to warm cookies, remove from sheet immediately with spatula and cool on racks. Dip side of cookie in melted chocolate, let set. Pipe lines of chocolate with paper cone, tip cut. Makes about one hundred.

SCHWARZE–STERNE
Black Stars

9 ounces confectioners' sugar
18 ounces sweet butter
4 eggs
1 teaspoon vanilla
25 ounces flour
½ teaspoon baking powder
¼ teaspoon salt
3½ ounces cocoa
½ teaspoon cinnamon

4 ounces English black currant preserves or other high-quality fruit preserves
1 cup tempered dark chocolate
Chocolate shot
Blanched almond halves

1. Mix well sugar, butter, eggs and vanilla by hand. Sift flour, baking powder, salt, cocoa and cinnamon together. Fold into first mixture. It is very important not to work the dough too much or butter will melt and cookies crack during baking. Refrigerate a half hour. Roll out to ⅛″ thickness, cut with small star cutter and bake at 350° about twelve minutes. Watch very carefully and test after ten minutes as cookies burn easily. Cool on racks.

2. Put preserves in paper cone with cut tip. Press out mound on one half of cookies, cover with remaining cookies. Dip tips of cookies in melted chocolate, then in chocolate shot. Let set. Pipe mound of chocolate in center of each cookie, garnish with almond half. Recipe makes about one hundred stars.

ZITRONENBLAETTER
Lemon Leaves

14 ounces sweet butter
7 ounces confectioners' sugar
4 egg yolks
Grated rind of two lemons
4 or 5 drops lemon flavoring
Juice of ½ lemon
Pinch of salt
20 ounces flour
Lemon Curd (recipe page 82)
4 ounces apricot preserves
½ cup tempered dark chocolate
1 cup Wilton Fondant (page 48) or Lemon Icing

1. Mix well all ingredients, except flour and salt. Combine flour and salt and mix by hand to a firm dough. Refrigerate one hour. Roll out to ⅛″ thickness, cut in leaf shapes. Bake on ungreased cookie sheets at 350° eight to ten minutes until golden.

2. Fill cookies with Lemon Curd. Refrigerate one hour. Brush tops with warm apricot glaze (heat jam to boiling and strain).

3. Warm fondant, tint with food color, and dip tops of cookies. Or dip in Lemon Icing. Let dry. Pipe veins and outlines of leaves with melted chocolate. Make rosette at base of each leaf and garnish with lemon peel. Recipe makes about one hundred leaves.

Lemon Icing

Juice of one lemon
about 1 cup confectioners' sugar
yellow food coloring

Mix lemon juice and sugar to very stiff paste. Add more sugar if needed. Tint. Warm over very low heat until just thin enough to dip cookies.

THE SPLENDID PLUM PUDDING SYMBOL OF CHRISTMAS CHEER

The rich, delicious plum pudding ablaze with brandy has been a highlight of the Christmas celebration in England for centuries.

Here is a moist, luscious Carrot Pudding that's ideal for families with small children, and a resplendent fruit-filled English Plum Pudding for more traditional dinners.

STEAMED CARROT PUDDING*

½ cup butter
1 cup sugar
2 cups finely chopped or ground carrots
1 cup finely chopped tart apples
2 cups sifted flour
1 teaspoon nutmeg
½ teaspoon cloves
1 teaspoon cinnamon
1 teaspoon baking soda
1 teaspoon vanilla
1 cup raisins (or 1 cup chopped dates)

1. Cream butter until fluffy, add sugar gradually and cream again. Stir in carrots and apples and mix well. Mix flour with the other dry ingredients, resift and add to the carrot-apple mixture. Mix well. Stir in vanilla and raisins (or dates).

2. Pour into well-buttered 1½-quart pudding mold. Cover, and seal the cover with butter. Place mold on trivet in a steamer or heavy kettle. Pour in boiling water, three-quarters of the way up the sides of the mold. Cover kettle or steamer tightly and steam at low heat an hour and a half. Garnish with candied cherries and serve warm with whipped cream, Hot Rum Sauce or Brandy Hard Sauce. Makes about twelve servings. (Note: This pudding may be frozen, then reheated by steaming as before.)

ENGLISH PLUM PUDDING*

This is an excellent example of the old-fashioned steamed puddings enjoyed in England. As Charles Dickens wrote in *A Christmas Carol*, "Oh, a wonderful pudding!" and your family will agree.

¾ cup dried currants
1 cup seedless raisins
1 cup white raisins
⅓ cup finely chopped candied fruit peel (mixed fruits)
⅓ cup candied cherries, finely chopped
½ cup slivered blanched almonds
1 small tart apple, cored and coarsely chopped
½ carrot, scraped and coarsely chopped
1 tablespoon finely grated orange peel
1 tablespoon finely grated lemon peel
¼ pound beef suet, finely chopped
1 cup flour
½ teaspoon ground allspice
½ teaspoon salt
2 cups fine crumbs of fresh white bread
½ cup dark brown sugar
3 eggs
½ cup brandy
¼ cup fresh orange juice
2 tablespoons fresh lemon juice
¼ cup brandy for flaming

1. Place the first eleven ingredients in a large bowl and stir them with your hands until well mixed.

2. Sift the flour with the allspice and salt and add to the fruit mixture. Mix well. Then add the bread crumbs and brown sugar and mix again.

3. In a separate bowl, beat the eggs until fluffy, add the one-half cup of brandy and the orange and lemon juice. Stir well. Pour this mixture over the fruit mixture and knead together with your hands until well blended. Cover with a damp towel and refrigerate at least twelve hours.

4. Butter one 2-quart pudding mold, spoon in the pudding, adjust cover and butter seams. (The English use a bowl-shaped mold without a cover and tie a floured cloth over the rim with a string.)

5. Put mold on a trivet in a large kettle and pour in boiling water, three-quarters of the way up sides of mold. Bring to a boil, cover kettle, reduce heat and simmer eight hours. Add more boiling water as needed.

6. Take pudding out of water, remove cover and cool to room temperature. Replace cover, or cover with foil, and refrigerate at least three weeks. (Plum puddings used to be made a year in advance and kept in a cool place for the following Christmas!)

7. To serve, place mold on trivet in kettle, pour in boiling water as before, cover the kettle, bring to a boil and simmer for two hours. Loosen sides with knife and invert on serving plate. Garnish with candied cherries and leaves of holly or ivy. To flame pudding, warm ¼ cup brandy, ignite and pour over pudding. Serve with mounds of Brandy Hard Sauce. Pipe tube 32 swirled mounds on cookie sheet, freeze until serving time. Serves twelve.

BRANDY HARD SAUCE*

½ cup butter
1½ cups confectioners' sugar
2 tablespoons brandy (or more, to taste)

Cream the butter until light and fluffy. Gradually beat in the sugar. Add the brandy, still beating. Chill before serving. To make stars for garnish, pipe tube 4B stars before chilling on back of cookie sheet and freeze. Remove from sheet, store in plastic bag.

HOT RUM SAUCE*

1 cup sugar
1 cup water
½ cup soft butter
¼ cup rum

Boil the sugar and water together until the syrup reaches the thread stage, 230°. Remove from heat, stir in the butter and, when that has melted, the rum. Serve immediately with plum pudding. Wonderful!

*From THE WILTON BOOK OF CLASSIC DESSERTS

Christmas treats of Ginger Bread

A happy holiday tradition is the custom of baking gingerbread. Everybody loves its spicy fragrance and delicious taste, and it's such fun to shape into centerpieces and cookies.

Use your favorite gingerbread or try Grandma's Gingerbread. One recipe makes the Christmas Dance with enough left over for place cards or cookies.

GRANDMA'S GINGERBREAD

5 to 5½ cups all-purpose flour
1 teaspoon baking soda
1 teaspoon salt
2 teaspoons ginger
2 teaspoons cinnamon
1 teaspoon nutmeg
1 teaspoon cloves
1 cup shortening
1 cup sugar
1¼ cups unsulphured molasses
2 eggs, beaten

1. Thoroughly mix flour, soda, salt and spices.

2. Melt shortening in large saucepan. Add sugar, molasses, and eggs; mix well. Cool slightly, then add four cups dry ingredients and mix well.

3. Turn mixture onto lightly floured surface. Knead in remaining dry ingredients by hand. Roll dough to ⅛″ thickness. Cut out pieces with cutters or knife. Place on greased cookie sheets with spatula.

4. Bake at 375° for eight to ten minutes depending on size. Let cool on cookie sheet a few minutes before removing to rack to cool completely.

MR. AND MRS. CLAUS

Welcome holiday guests with edible, take-home place cards. Just roll out dough ⅛″ thick, cut figures with 5″ gingerbread boy and girl cutters, and cut triangular supports with sharp knife. Bake, cool, then decorate with tube 2 and royal icing. Attach triangles to backs and fasten place cards and ribbons with icing. Half a cup of royal icing will trim six figures.

CHRISTMAS DANCE

Plan your holiday buffet around a jolly gingerbread centerpiece. You'll need one cup royal icing, food coloring, decorating tubes 2 and 4, decorating bag, round toothpicks, small gingerbread boy and girl cutters, 3″ star cutter, and patterns on page 94.

1. **Roll out dough,** cut an 8″ circular base, tree pieces, and nine each of gingerbread figures. Cut holes in tree sections with base of any standard decorating tube. Cut three stars with cutter. Leave one whole and cut other two in half. Trim ⅛″ off star halves along center. Bake gingerbread and cool. Smooth base of tree sections with sharp knife so tree will stand level.

2. **Decorate boys and girls** and front of star and tree pieces with tube 2 and royal icing. Dry two hours. Decorate backs of trees and stars. Dry two hours.

3. **Pipe tube 4 line of icing** down center of whole tree and inner edge of two half trees (see diagram, page 94). Join and prop at a 60-degree angle with balls of cotton and dry two hours. Attach two half stars to whole star with tube 2 line of icing. Prop with cotton and let dry two hours.

4. **Attach remaining half stars** to back of whole star the same way, attaching toothpick to base of star with icing. Attach half trees to back of whole tree, leaving tiny space at top to insert toothpick holding star. Pipe tube 2 beading along all seams.

5. **Set gingerbread base** on foil-covered cardboard circle and attach figures with dots of icing. Place star on tree, inserting toothpick into space at top. Pipe mound of icing on base and position tree.

HEART OF THE HOLIDAYS
THE CHRISTMAS CRECHE

A cherished tradition in many homes is the Christmas crèche, its beloved figures handed down from generation to generation. Why not start your own family tradition by baking a crèche of gingerbread?

You'll need the gingerbread recipe on page 90. One recipe makes enough for the crèche, with a little left over. Use the Really Big Cookie Cutter for trees, also animal cutters, small daisy and heart cutters, angel and star cutter from the Christmas Set, and small and large gingerbread people cutters, with the skirt of one figure trimmed to make St. Joseph's robe. You also need decorating tubes 1 and 10, decorating bags, 1½ cups royal icing, five cups boiled icing, edible glitter, food coloring, and spatula. Don't forget some brown candies to cover inside seams of the crèche, and cans to support it while it dries. To support the crèche, make a base of two 17"x10" pieces of cardboard, taped together and covered with foil.

1. Bake gingerbread and cut out cookies and pieces for crèche using patterns on page 94. When cool, outline the gingerbread people with tube 1 and fill in with thinned royal icing. Let dry at least three hours. Decorate figures, animals, star and trees with tube 1 and royal icing. Pipe tube 1 beading around heart "windows" on back walls. Allow trim to dry about three hours, then turn over. Attach two triangular braces on back of each large figure, one brace on back of animals with royal icing. Dry thoroughly.

2. Build crèche. Mark a line 2" in from each side of 16"x 9" base. This should be 3" from front of base and 2" from back. Pipe a tube 10 line of royal icing to hold side walls. Put the side walls on these lines, propping them with cans till set. At right angles, pipe two more tube 10 icing lines to secure back sections of wall. Put these pieces into place and prop them until set, at least one-half hour.

Now pipe a tube 10 line of icing along top of the side and back walls, and lay first one half of the roof and then the other on top, just to see where it should go. This will make an icing mark on inner part of roof. Pipe an additional line of icing over these marks, and pipe a line of icing along top seam on each roof section. Now set both halves of roof in place, and join seams at top. Have cans ready to prop ends of roof until icing sets firmly. Set a tall can inside the structure to support roof while it dries. While icing seams are wet, press in brown candies to cover them on inside of crèche. With royal icing, attach daisy pieces to back of crèche at corners where roof meets back walls.

3. Assemble figures, complete crèche. Ice base with boiled icing, swirling it with spatula to resemble snow. Leave area inside walls uncovered. Ice roof with boiled icing and make overhanging icicles with

Continued on page 94.

spatula. Sprinkle snow with edible glitter. Position figures and animals. Place trees against back of roof, and top with a little "snow". Attach star to front of roof, pressing it into the soft icing. Pipe dots of royal icing to attach Infant to Mary and Joseph. Pipe tube 10 ball border around gingerbread base.

If properly stored, the Christmas Crèche will last for years, making a permanent addition to your holiday celebration. Cover with airtight plastic wrap or seal in a plastic bag and store in a cool, dry place. It should not be frozen or refrigerated.

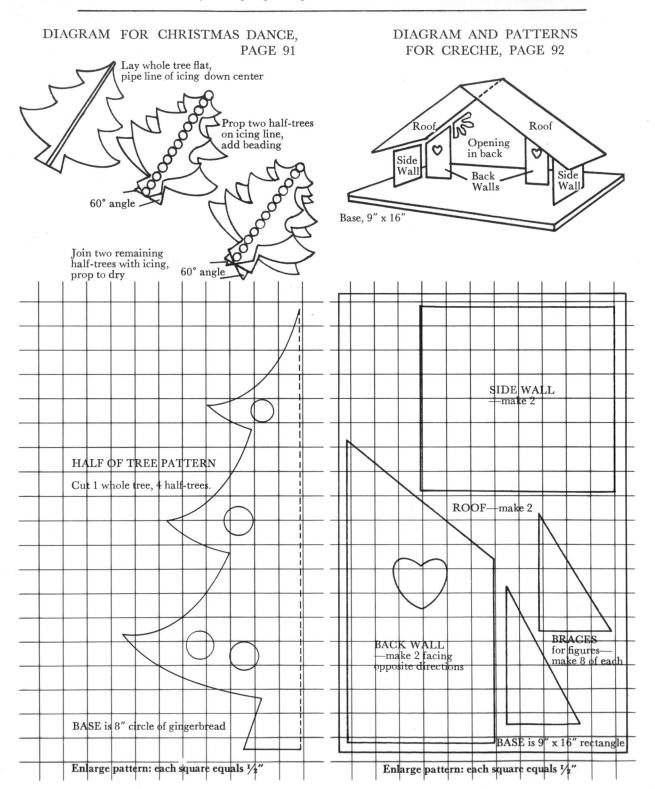

DIAGRAM FOR CHRISTMAS DANCE, PAGE 91

Lay whole tree flat, pipe line of icing down center

Prop two half-trees on icing line, add beading

60° angle

Join two remaining half-trees with icing, prop to dry

60° angle

HALF OF TREE PATTERN

Cut 1 whole tree, 4 half-trees.

BASE is 8" circle of gingerbread

Enlarge pattern: each square equals ½"

DIAGRAM AND PATTERNS FOR CRECHE, PAGE 92

Roof

Opening in back

Roof

Side Wall

Back Walls

Side Wall

Base, 9" x 16"

SIDE WALL —make 2

ROOF—make 2

BACK WALL —make 2 facing opposite directions

BRACES for figures— make 8 of each

BASE is 9" x 16" rectangle

Enlarge pattern: each square equals ½"

ICING RECIPES

These recipes have been tested and re-tested by Wilton and have proven to be both delicious and easy to handle in the decorating bag or cone. All can be mixed with a regular electric mixer. (Do not attempt to use a hand mixer.) If you are mixing a large quantity of icing, use a heavy-duty mixer such as the KitchenAid K5A, or a model with comparable power.

To thin icings for strings or leaves, add a little white corn syrup. Add one teaspoon per cup of icing for strings, two teaspoons per cup for leaves. Do not thin the Chocolate Buttercream Icing.

We have not given quantities of icing needed for various cakes, because usage varies greatly from decorator to decorator. About the only safe rule of thumb is four cups of any icing is sufficient to ice and completely decorate a 10″ round or an 8″ square cake. You will probably use less. Experience and practice will tell you how much icing you need.

We do not recommend using packaged icing mixes for borders or flowers. The made-at-home recipes here will give you better color and manageability.

Add liquid food color to icings for pastel tints. For deeper shades, use paste colors, sparingly.

WILTON BUTTERCREAM

A really Four-Star icing. Covers and handles well, and pipes fine flowers. If weather is not humid, pipe flowers in advance and air-dry. Or pipe the flowers and freeze them briefly for easy handling. Then place them on the cake shortly before serving. They will thaw in minutes.

    ⅓ cup butter
    ⅓ cup solid, white vegetable shortening
    1 teaspoon clear vanilla
    ⅛ teaspoon salt
    1 pound confectioners' sugar, sifted
    5 tablespoons cool milk or cream

Cream butter and shortening together with an electric mixer. Add vanilla and salt. Beat in sugar, 1 cup at a time, blending well after each addition and scraping sides and bottom of bowl with a spatula frequently. Add milk and beat at high speed until fluffy. Keep icing covered with lid or damp cloth and store in refrigerator. Bring to room temperature and rebeat to use again. Thin with corn syrup for strings and leaves. YIELD: 3 cups.

WILTON CHOCOLATE BUTTERCREAM

This is exceptionally good-tasting and easy to use.

Follow the recipe for Wilton Buttercream. First cream butter and shortening. Then add mixture of:
    ½ cup cocoa
    ½ cup milk
Proceed with the remainder of the recipe for Wilton Buttercream above. Store in the refrigerator until ready to use, bring to room temperature and rebeat. Stiffen with a little confectioners' sugar for piping flowers. Do not thin for making leaves. For a very dark color, add one or two drops of brown food coloring. Yield: 3⅔ cups.

WILTON SNOW-WHITE BUTTERCREAM

This will be your choice for wedding cakes, or any cake where a pure white appearance is important.
    ⅔ cup water
    4 tablespoons meringue powder
    1¼ cups solid white shortening, room temperature
    ¾ teaspoon salt
    ¼ teaspoon butter flavoring
    ½ teaspoon almond flavoring
    ½ teaspoon clear vanilla flavoring
    11½ cups sifted confectioners' sugar
Combine water and meringue powder and whip at high speed until peaks form. Add four cups sugar, one cup at a time, beating after each addition at low speed. Alternately add shortening and remainder of sugar. Add salt and flavorings and beat at low speed until smooth. Thin with two teaspoons of white corn syrup for leaves and strings. Yield: 8 cups. Recipe may be cut in half or doubled.

WILTON BOILED ICING—MERINGUE

A fine, easy to use, pure white icing for flowers and borders. Dries too crisp for covering the cake.
    4 level tablespoons Wilton Meringue Powder
    1 cup warm water
    2 cups granulated sugar
    ¼ teaspoon cream of tartar
    3½ cups sifted confectioners' sugar
Boil granulated sugar, ½ cup water and cream of tartar to 240°. Brush side of pan with warm water to keep crystals from forming. Meanwhile, mix meringue powder with ½ cup water, beat 7 minutes at high speed. Turn to low speed, add confectioners' sugar, beat 4 minutes at high speed. Slowly add boiled sugar mixture, beat 5 minutes at high speed.

Keeps a week in refrigerator, covered with damp cloth. Rebeat before using again. Yield: 6 cups. Do not double recipe, unless you use a heavy-duty mixer.

Continued on next page

BATTER AND BAKING CHART

Here is a Batter and Baking Chart prepared by Culinary Arts Institute. Pillsbury mixes with Grade A Large eggs were used, tested and re-tested.

Culinary Arts found that the yellow cake mix produced six cups of batter. This mix was also closest in texture, appearance and volume to a "scratch" (not a "mix") cake. Most two-egg cake recipes produce six cups of batter, but some do vary.

Banana flavor mix yields only 4½ cups of batter. However it rises more than the yellow cake mix, so in estimating the batter that will fill a pan, use about 25% less batter than listed in the chart.

All baking times are for preheated 350° oven

Pan	Size	Cups of Batter	Minutes to bake
ROUND (2″ deep)	6″*	2¼	25-35
	8″	4½	35-45
	10″	6½	40-50
	12″	9	40-50
	14″	12	45-55
	16″	15½	45-55
	18″	18	45-55
SQUARE (2″ deep)	6″	3	25-35
	8″	5	30-40
	10″	8	35-45
	12″	11½	30-40
	14″	15½	35-45
	16″	17½	35-45
	18″	21	35-45
PETAL (2″ deep)	6″	1¾	30-40
	9″	4	35-45
	12″	7½	40-50
	15″	13	40-50
HEART (2″ deep)	6″	2½	25-35
	9″	4	30-40
	12″	9	30-40
	15″	13	40-50
HEXAGON (2″ deep)	6″	1½	25-35
	9″	3½	30-40
	12″	8	35-45
	15″	13	40-50
RECTANGLE (2″ deep)	9″x13″	8½	35-45
	11″x15″	12½	35-45
	12″x18″	16	40-50
LONG LOAF (4¼″ deep)	16″x4″	10 or one angel food mix	55-65
LITTLE LOAFERS (1½″ deep)	4⅜″x2½″	½ each pan	20-25
BALL PAN	6″ diam.	2½ each pan half	40-50
SMALL WONDER MOLDS	3½″ diam.	¾ each mold	20-30
LARGE WONDER MOLD		6	50-55
HEXAGON RING		5	35-40
TURK'S HEAD		4½	35-40

*For a 6″ layer, 1½″ high, use 1½ cups of batter.

ICING Continued

WILTON BOILED ICING—EGG WHITE

A good-flavored, snow-white icing suitable for covering the cake. Borders are not quite as clear and detailed as when made with meringue boiled icing. Do not use for flowers.

2 cups granulated sugar
½ cup water
¼ teaspoon cream of tartar
4 egg whites (room temperature)
1½ cups confectioners' sugar, measured then sifted

Boil granulated sugar, water, cream of tartar to 240°. Brush sides of pan with warm water to prevent crystals. Brush again halfway through, but do not stir. Meanwhile, whip egg whites seven minutes at high speed. Add boiled sugar mixture slowly, beat three minutes at high speed. Turn to second speed, gradually add confectioners' sugar, beat seven minutes more at high speed. Rebeating won't restore texture. Yield: 3½ cups. Unless using a heavy-duty mixer, do not double recipe.

WILTON ROYAL ICING—MERINGUE

A durable, hard-drying icing very useful for "glueing" decorated pieces. Not for covering cakes, as it is much too hard when dry. It does make sharp, perfect borders and trims and realistic "souvenir" flowers. Perfect for "dummy" cakes, used only for display.

A heavy-duty mixer will produce a better royal icing, but home mixer can be used. Do not double the recipe unless you are using a heavy-duty mixer.

3 level tablespoons Wilton Meringue Powder
1 pound confectioners' sugar
3½ ounces warm water
½ teaspoon cream of tartar

Combine ingredients, mixing slowly, then beat at high speed for seven to ten minutes. Keep covered at all times with damp cloth, as icing dries very quickly. To restore texture after storing, simply rebeat. Yield: 3½ cups.

WILTON ROYAL ICING—EGG WHITE

An even harder icing than the meringue royal icing, above. Use for the same purposes.

3 egg whites (room temperature)
1 pound confectioners' sugar
½ teaspoon cream of tartar

Combine ingredients, beat at high speed for 7 to 10 minutes. Very quick-drying; keep covered with damp cloth. Rebeating will not restore. Yields 3 cups.

The tools, tubes and pans needed to create the decorated pieces in this book may be purchased in many retail stores or through the Wilton YEARBOOK. Write to Wilton Enterprises, Inc. 2240 West 75th Street, Woodridge, Illinois 60515.